CHEVROLET

YESTERDAY & TODAY™

THE AUTO EDITORS OF CONSUMER GUIDE®

Publications International, Ltd.

ISBN-13: 978-1-60553-337-7
ISBN-10: 1-60553-337-8

Manufactured in China.

8 7 6 5 4 3 2 1

Library of Congress Control Number: 2010921975

Credits

Photography:

The editors would like to thank the following people and organizations for supplying the photography that made this book possible. They are listed below, along with page number(s) of their photos.

Chan Bush: 12, 68; Gary Cameron: 148; Jeff Cohn: 99; Thomas Glatch: 78, 82; David Gooley: 16; Sam Griffith: 13, 19, 46, 54, 63, 66, 118, 129, 135, 137, 147, 148; Jerry Heasley: 42, 104, 109; Don Heiny: 22; Brandon Hemphill: 78, 94, 119; Gary Johns: 47; Jeff Johnson: 14; Bud Juneau: 43, 99, 115; Milton Kieft: 15, 95, 117; Nick Komic: 75, 98, 99, 107; Dan Lyons: 15, 69, 72, 86, 146; Vince Manocchi: 14, 15, 16, 40, 41, 45, 47, 51, 53, 57, 63, 77, 94, 101, 109, 112, 113, 114, 116, 117, 118, 119, 120, 122, 123, 136, 139; Roger Mattingly: 62, 76, 96; Doug Mitchel: 25, 26, 49, 55, 67, 69, 70, 71, 72, 79, 82, 83, 98, 100, 101, 108, 114, 120, 135, 141, 142, 147, 149; Mike Mueller: 52, 100, 105, 109, 113, 158; Bob Nicholson: 74; Nina Padgett: 121, 128; Jay Peck: 158; E.T. Satory Collection: 81, 84, 145; Tom Shaw: 21; Gary Smith: 11, 29; Mike Spenner: 38, 39; Richard Spiegelman: 18; Steve Statham: 148; Tom Storm: 86; David Temple: 24, 28, 69, 117, 149, 153; Bob Tenney: 84; Phil Toy: 83, 99, 106; W. C. Waymack: 17, 18, 20, 44, 50, 52, 56, 73, 84, 114, 146, 147, 149, 158, 159; White Eagle Studios: 153; Nicky Wright: 43, 67, 105

Owners:

Special thanks to the owners of the cars featured in this book for their cooperation.

Mark Alter: 122; Barbara Ann: 20; John J. Appelhanz: 38, 39; Jim and Mary Ashworth: 43; Orville L. Baer: 159; Howard L. Baker: 117; John Baritel: 118; Nelson Bates: 149; Jim Blanchard: 114; Bill Borland: 83; James and Patricia Boyk: 153; Jeanine and Don Brink: 56; Bill Bush: 53; Jim Cahill: 46; Stephen Capone: 69; Joe Carfagna: 22; Dorothy Clemmer: 112; Contemporary and Investment Auto: 158; Corvette Mike: 123; Allen Cummins: 119; Rick Cybul: 109; David Dawes and Bob Painter: 95; Richard and Joyce Dollmeyer: 55; Greg Don: 109; Steve Donnell/Donnell Body Shop: 42; Bill Edman: 159; Douglas Englin: 82; David Ertel: 21; Rex and Justin Fager: 146; Gordon A. Fenner: 28; David L. Ferguson: 112; Don Ferry: 76; Bob Flack: 67; John L. Fuller: 52; Mr. and Mrs. Raymond Garcia: 12; Paul Garlick: 148; George W. Gass: 84; Jack Gersh: 120; William Giembroniewicz: 146; Dave and Mary Glass: 118; Jaime H. Gonzales: 72; Eric P. Goodman: 114; Bill Grathic: 86; Howard Gumbel: 147; Bill Halliday: 16; Charles M. Havelka: 135; William T. Hayes and sons: 17; Lloyd Heniger: 11; Dorene Hofberg: 79; Tony Hossain: 75; Royce Hudgins II: 24; Jeff Hyosaka: 106; Illinois State Police Department: 141; J. Bruce Jacobs: 116; John E. and Barbara E. James/World of Wheels: 121; Roger A. James: 14;

Blaine Jenkins: 43; Bill Jones: 115; Robert Kleckauskas: 118; Mike Knecht: 99; Terry Knight: 147; Bill and Diann Kohley: 147; Edward S. Kuziel: 113; Donald Laraway: 146; Wayne and Pat Lasley: 44; Charley Lillard: 99; Phillip and Sandy LoPiccolo: 116; Los Angeles Police Historical Society: 136; Terry Lucas: 51; Ron Lynch: 77; Joseph and Suzanne Lysy: 71; Jim MacDonald: 83; Bob Macy: 104, 109; Donald Maich: 115; Bill and Rita Malik: 47; Jack and Jan Matske: 67; Dick McKean: 15; Tom Meleo: 15; Andrew J. Mesrausras: 83; Marty Meza: 94; Jim Miller: 57; Paul F. Miller: 14; Mr. and Mrs. Richard D. Miller: 105; Connie and Larry Mitchell: 74; Ann M. Mocklin: 101; Bob Moore: 70; Motor Cars, Ltd.: 69; Ronald S. Mroz: 76, 96; Jerrold V. Murphy: 78; John Murray: 63; Danny L. Naile: 149; Northwest Auto Sales: 94, 119; Louis and Inez Nosse: 15; John R. Oehler: 98, 100; Edward E. Ortiz: 123; Ray Ostrander: 45; Dr. Dennis Pagliano: 113; John W. Petras: 49, 66; George Pointer: 135; John Poochigian: 40, 41; Arthur Rathburn: 29; Lloyd and Karen Ray: 69; Danny Reed: 117; Greg Reynolds: 137; Vivian Riley: 71; Ron and Laureen Roach: 99; John Rowling: 158; James A. Ruby: 86; Jeff Ruppert: 108; Lydia and Byron Ruetten: 149; Rod Ryan: 82; Joseph F. Salierno: 153; Tom Schay: 116; Bill Schoenbeck: 13, 19; Steve Schultz/SS Classic Cars: 98, 99, 107; Bill Schwelitz: 50; Dale Shetley: 139; Jerry Shumate: 158; Raymond Silva, Jr.: 16; Mary and Marshall Simpkin: 18; Roy L. Spencer: 84; Charles E. Stinson: 52; Tom and Nancy Stump: 105; Andrew Surmeier: 17; Chuck Swafford: 115; Larry and Loretta Swedberg: 26; Steve Sydell: 54; Marion and Lindy VanWormer: 72; Carlos and Sherry Vivas: 117; David Voegele: 25; Barry Waddell: 100; Donald Walkemeyer: 20; Rosalie and Jim Wente: 114; William A. Whitney: 68; Bobby Wiggins: 63, 149; Karl Wilke: 62; Henry Woodrow: 73; Bill Worthington: 158; Mike and Laurie Yager: 120

Our appreciation to the historical archives and media services groups at General Motors Company.

About The Auto Editors of Consumer Guide®:

For more than 40 years, Consumer Guide® has been a trusted provider of new-car buying information.

The Consumer Guide® staff drives and evaluates more than 200 vehicles annually.

Consumerguide.com is one of the Web's most popular automotive resources, visited by roughly three million shoppers monthly.

The Auto Editors of Consumer Guide® also publish the award-winning bimonthly *Collectible Automobile*® magazine.

Contents

Foreword

Welcome to *Chevrolet: Yesterday and Today*™, a pictorial tribute to an American institution beloved as much as...well, baseball, hot dogs, and apple pie, to quote the old ad slogan. Countless millions have owned a Chevrolet car or truck at one time or another. And people keep coming back to the "bowtie" brand year after year, even in the turbulent times of the early 21st century. No doubt about it: Chevrolet is one of the most successful nameplates in automotive history and a name now known and respected around the world.

Like many cultural icons, Chevrolet means different things to different people. For some, it's childhood memories of a faithful sedan or station wagon that was often regarded as part of the family. For others, it's the excitement of a racy Corvette sports car, the "happy days" nostalgia of a classic 1955-57 Bel Air, or the power and pizzazz of a big Impala or midsize Malibu from the go-go 1960s. Others think of Chevrolet as the only truck brand they'd ever consider buying. And, of course, there are millions of racing fans loyal to Chevrolet, especially devotees of NASCAR stock-car competition.

It's this multifaceted brand personality that gave us the idea of organizing *Chevrolet: Yesterday and Today*™ around body styles and vehicle types instead of taking a straight chronological

Although considered a 1913 model, the first production Chevrolet left the factory in late 1912. Chevrolet was named for racing driver Louis Chevrolet (right), who designed the first Chevy.

approach like most automotive histories. We think you'll find this presentation both fun and enlightening. It certainly helped us to appreciate anew that while no nameplate can be all things to all people, Chevrolet comes as close as any.

In fairness, the above comments also apply to Chevrolet's perennial archrival Ford, another make whose impressive success in the early 20th century was built with sturdy, dependable, and affordable vehicles designed for America's fast-growing middle class. One key distinction, however, is that Chevrolet has been the nation's top-selling car and truck brand far longer than Ford. In fact, Chevy reigned supreme as "USA-1" in most every year from 1927 all the way through the early 1980s.

A key factor in Chevy's rise during the 1920s and '30s was being part of General Motors, the automaker whose mastery of design, engineering, and marketing made it the unassailable U.S. industry leader by the 1940s and, by some measures, the world's largest corporation. But let's not forget that GM likely wouldn't have become so huge and influential had it not been for the consistent popularity of Chevrolet cars and trucks.

That, in turn, reflects the fact that Chevrolet always got as much attention as any other GM brand—and sometimes more. Though GM might introduce a technical or styling innovation on ritzy Cadillacs, Chevrolet models usually got it within two or three years. Examples include all-steel "Turret Top" construction, four-wheel coil-spring suspension, fully automatic Powerglide transmission, and "hardtop" styling—to name a few.

And unusually for a mass-market brand, Chevrolet has had its share of industry firsts. The sporty Corvette, for example, pioneered the use of fiberglass bodies in sustained, regular production. And Chevy's all-new 1955 "small-block" V-8 has long been regarded as an engineering landmark, imitated by rival brands but never bettered. No wonder it's been such a longtime performance favorite among hot-rodders and even for a few boutique European automakers. Other innovations, like the rear-engine Corvair compact car, were too radical or flawed to sell the way GM had planned, but the flops were rare and never fatal, given Chevy's continuing strong success overall.

Things are different today. Thanks to decades of corporate drift and denial, plus unprecedented foreign competition, changing consumer tastes, and other factors, Chevrolet is now well down the list in U.S. car sales. And Ford has been number-one in trucks since 1980. Fortunately for its many fans, Chevy seems poised for a comeback, symbolized by the groundbreaking 2011 Volt extended-range plug-in hybrid, a potentially game-changing electric vehicle for a new age with many new and vexing challenges.

The bowtie brand has certainly come a long way since its founding nearly 100 years ago by the talented Louis Chevrolet and the wily William C. "Billy" Durant, who folded the company into General Motors barely four years after the very first Chevy prototype was built. It's a fascinating story, and we hope you enjoy learning about it in the following pages.

CHAPTER ONE

Family Haulers

Flashy hardtop coupes and convertibles may get all the glory, but sensible sedans and station wagons have historically been an automaker's real bread and butter. Chevrolet has long excelled at producing these no-nonsense, value-oriented machines—vehicles that sold almost entirely on their practical virtues. Though they may not have been quite as glamorous as their sportier siblings, General Motors designers usually managed to infuse even the most plain-Jane Chevys with a decent amount of eye-catching style. And over the years, these mainstream family movers were typically available with the same industry-leading technological features—trend-setting advancements such as "Turret Top" all-steel roofs, "Powerglide" automatic transmissions, and flow-through "Astro Ventilation."

Big Chevy wagons lost their separate model names for 1962, but remained four-doors available with six- or nine-passenger seating. This Bel Air started at $2819 with the standard six-cylinder engine.

1925-1927

Left: *Shown here is a body-drop station in a Chevrolet assembly plant. Wood artillery wheels were standard equipment on Chevy's open cars in 1925, while the closed coupes and sedans came with steel disc wheels.*

Like many automakers, Chevrolet was on a roll in the mid-Twenties. In 1925, Chevy sales increased by a whopping 70 percent, and the company celebrated the production of its two-millionth car. In 1927, Ford Motor Company shut down production lines for five months to change over from Model T production to the new Model A; this helped Chevrolet outsell Ford for the first time. Meanwhile, the popularity of open cars was fading drastically. The three top-selling 1927 Chevys were the Coach, the Coupe, and the Sedan—all closed-body-style cars.

Right and below: *The most popular Chevrolet for 1927 was the Coach two-door sedan, which started at $695. Production hit a healthy 239,566.*

Far right: *The $715 Capitol Series AA Sports Cabriolet, featured here in a 1927 Country Life magazine ad, was built to look like a convertible, but it actually had a fixed-position top. It was the first Chevrolet (and in fact, the first low-priced car of any make) to be furnished with a rumble seat.*

MAY, 1927   COUNTRY LIFE   93

for Economical Transportation
CHEVROLET

ALL the distinction, elegance and luxury of marvelous new bodies by Fisher . . . All the smoothness, handling ease and dependability of Chevrolet's proved and modern design, enhanced by scores of important mechanical improvements . . . And, too, amazing new low prices. It is easy to understand why a new vogue is sweeping America—the vogue of the Most Beautiful Chevrolet in Chevrolet History.

Touring or Roadster $525, Coach $595, Coupe $625, Sedan $695, Sport Cabriolet $715,
Landau $745. Balloon tires standard equipment on all models. All prices f. o. b. Flint, Michigan
CHEVROLET MOTOR COMPANY, DETROIT, MICHIGAN
Division of General Motors Corporation

QUALITY AT LOW COST

1935-1938

Chevrolet pioneered several new features for low-priced cars in the mid-Thirties. "Knee-Action" independent front suspension debuted for 1934. For 1935, all-steel "Turret Top" roofs were introduced, but only on top-line Master DeLuxe models. Previous closed cars used wood and fabric inserts in their tops, but GM's Turret Top models had one-piece steel roofs—an advancement made possible by the advent of larger sheetmetal dies and stamping machinery. Four-wheel hydraulic brakes bowed for 1936 and were standard on all Chevys; Ford wouldn't match this feature for another three years.

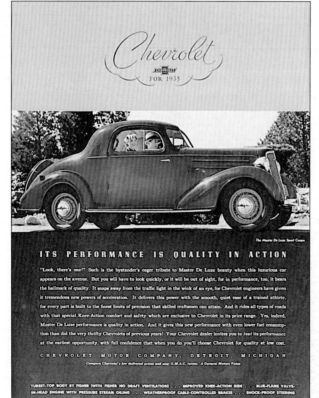

Right: *Rumble-seat coupes could serve as family haulers in a pinch. This ad, appearing in* The Saturday Evening Post *of June 1, 1935, spotlights the rumble-seat three-window Sport Coupe in the uplevel Master DeLuxe line.*

Above: *Like all Standard-line 1935 Chevys, the $550 four-door sedan wore warmed-over 1934 styling.* **Left:** *The fanciful hood ornament had a stylized "winged seahorse" motif.*

Left: *Inside, the '35 Standards retained a 1933-style instrument panel, but boasted nice interior fittings for a low-priced car.*

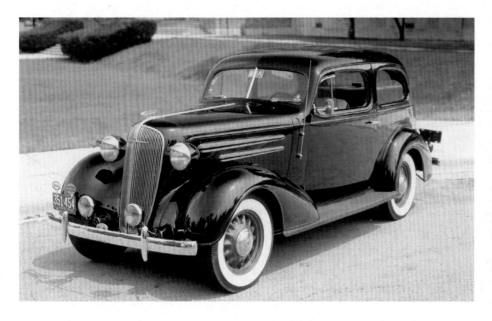

Left: *The 1936 Standard dashboards were rather spartan affairs with simple controls. Note the steering-column-mounted fan.*

Below: *In-car audio was quite a luxury in the Thirties. Chevrolet's 1938 accessories catalog tempted shoppers with these art-deco radios.*

Above: *The 1936 Chevrolets wore a unique "fencer's mask" grille, as seen on this Standard Town Sedan.* **Right:** *This 1937 Chevy ad pressed the comfort and safety of optional Knee-Action independent front suspension, which was still reserved for top-line cars.*

1941-1948

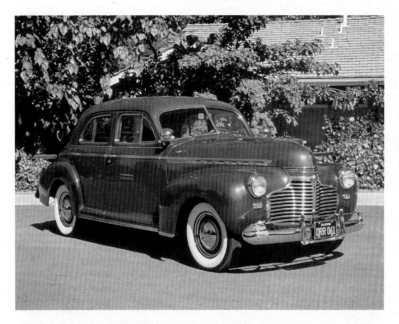

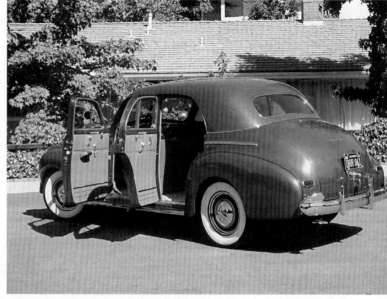

Right and far right: *Outside of the $949 convertible and $995 "woodie" station wagon, the $877 Special DeLuxe Fleetline four-door sedan was the priciest 1941 Chevrolet.*

Right: *After the attack on Pearl Harbor, the U.S. government began restricting the civilian use of strategic materials such as chrome and stainless steel. This Fleetline Aerosedan is typical of the resulting "blackout specials," which were built in January and early February 1942.*

Above: *Holding the top rung on Chevrolet's price ladder for 1947 was the Fleetmaster station wagon, an eight-passenger four-door with a structural wood body. It started at $1893.*

The 1941 model year brought eye-catching new styling, a three-inch-longer wheelbase, and numerous technical improvements to the Chevrolet passenger-car line. But the expanding war in Europe, and America's subsequent entry into the fight, would soon put automotive innovations on hold for Chevrolet and all other American carmakers. After a limited run of 1942-model vehicles, civilian industrial production ended as U.S. factories geared up to assist the war effort. Chevrolet's first postwar vehicles rolled out for the 1946 model year, and were basically '42s with minor styling changes. The 1947 and '48 models were likewise facelifted prewar designs, but after a three-year drought of no new vehicles, it didn't matter much to the American buying public. Shoppers snapped up new vehicles as fast as the automakers could produce them, and Chevy sales soared.

Above: *This 1948 Fleetline Aerosedan wears several popular accessories of the period, including spotlights, bumper guards, window shades, and a sun visor.* **Left:** *The $1492 Fleetline Sportmaster four-door sedan garnered 64,217 orders for 1948.*

1949-1950

Above: *This 1949 Fleetline DeLuxe four-door sedan is dressed up with headlamp shades, windshield visor, wheel trim rings, and white-wall tires.*

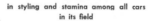

FIRST

in styling and stamina among all cars
in its field

You want your car to *look* and *act* the part of a leader in every phase of its design, engineering and performance. And you want it to *keep on looking and acting* the part of a leader, day after day, month after month, and year after year. So do millions of other motorists, and that's one vital reason why they prefer Chevrolet and continue to buy Chevrolet again and again, giving it the *highest rate of owner loyalty* of any car manufactured today, according to a recent independent nationwide survey. Owner after owner will tell you Chevrolet is first in styling and stamina among all cars in its field!

and FINEST

in all-round performance with economy
from two great engines

Yes, this thrilling new Chevrolet for '50 is the *only* low-priced car that offers you a choice of two great Valve-in-Head engines as well as two great drives. You may have the new Chevrolet 105-h.p. Valve-in-Head engine, offered in combination with the Powerglide automatic transmission—the *most powerful* engine in its field. Or you may have the highly improved, more powerful standard Chevrolet Valve-in-Head engine, offered in combination with the famous Silent Synchro-Mesh Transmission. Both of them are *outstanding* for all-round performance with economy! *Combination of Powerglide automatic transmission and 105-h.p. engine optional on De Luxe models at extra cost.*

at LOWEST COST

all these finer features cost you less
than in any other car

Left: *The 1950 Chevrolets saw only minor styling changes, including a slightly revamped grille.*

Above: *The fastback styling of late-Forties/ early-Fifties Chevys would soon fall out of favor; hardtop styling was just around the corner.*

Chevrolet's first all-new postwar vehicles debuted for 1949. The new bodies brought numerous interior improvements, including an asymmetric dash design and wider doors. In addition, all seats were moved forward so that rear passengers no longer rode above the rear axle. This meant more hip room as well as "a safer, softer, roomier ride that cradles you between the wheels—plus sensational handling qualities," according to Chevrolet ad copy. The 1950 models were largely carried over with minor changes, but sales still set a new record at nearly 1.5 million units. The continued sales success was probably helped by the line's clear styling kinship to more-expensive GM cars.

Left: *Repeating as Chevy's single most-popular model for 1950 was the $1520 Styleline DeLuxe Sport Sedan, which attracted a smashing 316,412 orders.*

Right: *Powerglide transmissions debuted as an option for 1950. Though it sapped acceleration, Powerglide was the first fully automatic transmission available in a low-priced car.*

1953-1954

Left: *Even the pedestrian four-door-sedan body style could look plenty flashy in top-line Bel Air trim, especially when the optional two-tone paint was selected. This example wears India Ivory over Horizon Blue. The four-door sedan was easily the best-selling 1953 Bel Air model, with 247,284 produced.*

Right: *This "family portrait" highlights the newly revamped 1953 Chevy lineup with three trim levels: a base group called One-Fifty, midlevel Two-Ten, and top-line Bel Air.* **Far right:** *Chevy wagon offerings grew from one to three for 1953, all four-doors. Pictured is the $2123 six-passenger Two-Ten Handyman.*

Above: *This brochure touted the features and benefits of Chevy's power steering, a new option for '53.* **Below:** *Much of Chevrolet's 1954 print advertising portrayed small-town America.*

assenger Chevys were fully restyled for 1953 around the same 115-inch-wheelbase chassis and basic inner bodies of the 1949–52 models. Begun under GM designer Ed Glowacke but completed under new Chevy styling chief Clare MacKichan, the 1953 facelift considerably freshened the division's 1949-vintage body design. A "toothy" grille provided a visual link to the new Corvette sports car, and Bel Airs had a lot of new brightwork all around. For 1954, a minor styling update brought a revised grille with two extra "teeth," oval outboard parking lamps, and fluted headlight rims. Chevy sales were down overall for '54, in part because a brand-new design was being rumored for 1955, but also because of a brutal price war touched off by a Ford production blitz.

Left: *Styling and color choices were becoming more important than ever in the early Fifties. Color swatches and scale models helped stylists map out the options in their model lineups.*

Left: *"Smooth lines and smarter styling" was how Chevy billed its modestly facelifted '54s. Shown here is the $1884 Bel Air four-door sedan.*

1955-1957

The 1955–57 "tri-five" Chevys were revolutionary cars that brought a whole new level of head-turning style and exhilarating performance to the division. Highlights of the all-new 1955 design included a Ferrari-esque "eggcrate" grille, and tasteful chrome trim that looked great with two-tone paint. Though six-cylinder power was still available, the big news under the hood was the all-new "Turbo-Fire" V-8—Chevrolet's first modern V-8 engine. For 1956, a heavy facelift brought a bulkier front-end design, new taillights, and swoopier trim, while the V-8 got more power and a "Super Turbo-Fire" moniker. Even-flashier bodywork debuted for 1957 and included a mesh grille, twin "gun-sight" hood ornaments, and bigger tailfins. The 1955–57 Chevys' iconic styling and solid engineering have earned them a place among history's most-celebrated cars.

Below: *The 1956 Chevrolets received a heavy facelift. Two-Ten four-door sedans, like this Nassau Blue/India Ivory example, edged out the four-door Bel Air as the most popular Chevy.*

Above: *Staged studio shots were often used in the Fifties to glamorize workaday products like the $1728 One-Fifty four-door sedan.* **Right:** *Two-Ten models offered a bit more pizzazz, especially when equipped with the optional bumper guards. Delray club coupes like this one sold for $1835 in 1955.*

Right: *Even in wagon form, the glamorous 1957 Chevrolets dazzled. The Two-Ten Townsman was the most popular of the lot, attracting almost 128,000 orders at a base price of $2456.*

1959

The automotive styling race of the Fifties reached its peak at the end of the decade, as Detroit automakers tried to outdo each other with increasingly radical designs. Outlandish "bat-wing" fins and "cat-eye" taillights were the most prominent (and polarizing) elements of the 1959 Chevy's styling. The look was a bit less dramatic up front, where horizontal "nostrils" at the leading edge of the hood ducted air into the engine compartment. The growth between 1957 and 1959 was amazing: length up by nearly 11 inches, width by seven inches, weight by 300 pounds. Clearly, even buyers of low-priced cars in the late Fifties were guided by the "bigger is better" mantra. The model lineup now ascended through Biscayne, Bel Air, and top-line Impala models, along with corresponding station-wagon trim levels Brookwood, Parkwood, Kingswood, and Nomad.

Below: *All 1959 GM cars sported a lot more glass, but awkwardly angled windshield pillars still hindered graceful entry and exit. Chevy's PR department recommended the technique shown here.*

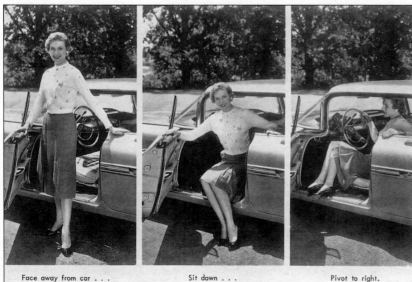

Face away from car . . .   Sit down . . .   Pivot to right.

Above and left: *With Impala ascending to Chevy's top rung, Bel Air became the mid-range series for '59. Shown here is the $2440 four-door sedan in Frost Blue.*

One of 5 Chevy wagons—the Brookwood with seats for six and Safety <u>Plate</u> Glass all around.

Bottom: *This Biscayne four-door sedan shows how Chevy's much-wider '59 bodies left wheels well inboard, creating a look that one stylist termed "a football player in ballet slippers."*

CHEVY holds everybody and his brother—beautifully! Busy people find the roominess of a Chevrolet wagon made to order. Especially people with little kids to consider. You can tote a whole swarm of Brownies or Cubs. There's 90 cubic feet of cargo space in all 5 Chevy wagons. You might prefer the 9-passenger job with its rear-facing third seat. But whether it's a wagon or a sedan or a convertible you go for, Chevrolet's roomier Fisher Body seats you in style. Some evening after a hectic day drop by your Chevrolet dealer's and just sit in one.

CHEVROLET THE CAR THAT'S WANTED FOR ALL ITS WORTH • CHEVROLET DIVISION OF GENERAL MOTORS, DETROIT 2, MICHIGAN

1961

Along with their corporate siblings, Chevy's totally redesigned 1961 "standards" were the first General Motors cars to bear the full imprint of corporate design chief Bill Mitchell, who had taken over GM styling in 1959. The result was a cleaner, more coherent big Chevy that was 1.5 inches shorter, yet looked much trimmer despite an unchanged 119-inch wheelbase. The chassis used the same "X-frame" layout as before, but Chevrolet claimed that the '61 models provided "the most quiet, vibration-dampened, relaxing ride you've ever tried."

Left: *Base engine in the '61 full-size Chevys remained the trusty "Blue Flame" inline six. It produced 135 horsepower from its 235.5 cubic inches.*

Left: *The base Brookwood four-door station wagon, shown here in Laguna Blue, retailed for $2653 with six-cylinder power or $2760 with a V-8.*

Right: *The '61 pillared sedans, like this Bel Air two-door, took over the overhanging rear roof and big wrapped window from previous Chevy sport sedan hardtops. All big '61 Chevys featured a more convenient bumper-height trunk opening.*

Left: *Keeping in step with the more subdued bodywork, interiors were toned down this year. Note the center-mounted glovebox and horizontal speedometer.*

1968-1969

Above: *The Impala wagon continued in six- and nine-passenger versions and started at $3245. The standard V-8 for all 1968 big Chevys was now a more-emissions-friendly 307 small-block with 200 hp.*

After a striking 1967 redesign with volup-tuous "Coke-bottle" curves, the 1968 big Chevys got a thorough facelift along the same styl-ing themes. Again, the "longer, lower, and wider" mantra prevailed; overall length was increased by as much as 1.7 inches. Interiors were also upgraded—all 1968 models were generally more plush inside. For 1969, Chevys gained a burly new look that featured prominent bulges around the wheels and massive loop-style front and rear bum-pers. New flow-through "Astro Ventilation" elimi-nated the need for front-door vent windows.

Below: *Biscayne sedans again anchored the big-Chevy line for '68. Six-cylinder versions retained a 250-cubic-inch engine with 155 hp, as did counterpart Bel Air models, which were only a bit fancier.*

Impala Custom Coupe

Ridiculously reasonable.

There are cars that would ask you to stick out your financial neck for what an Impala has.

For the money you get a huge body. A huge trunk. Huge coil springs at every wheel.

For the money you get a key that locks the ignition, steering wheel and transmission lever in one fell swoop.

For the money you get fenders inside fenders to fight rust and rocker panels that let out water and suck in air to fight rust.

For the money you get the entire front end of your car protected by a one-piece bumper.

For the money you get Astro Ventilation, a steel "guard rail" strengthening every door.

There isn't another car in this whole wide world that gives you all that, for the money.

Putting you first, keeps us first.

Above: *The 1969 Impala Custom Coupe started at a "ridiculously reasonable" $3085.*

1971-1974

Left: *Chevrolet's big 1971 wagons featured a new "Glide-Away" lift-gate/tailgate resembling a cross between a clamshell and a roll-top desk. As shown on this Kingswood Estate, the push of a button retracted the rear window into the roof and the tailgate under the cargo floor.*

The American auto industry was forced to contend with a whole new raft of challenges as the Seventies progressed. Increasing levels of government regulation brought mandates such as the Clean Air Act of 1970, which spurred GM to detune its 1971 engines to run on unleaded fuel. Bumpers began getting larger and more prominent for 1973, when the National Highway Traffic Safety Administration enacted regulations requiring "5-mph" bumpers that could withstand low-speed impacts with no functional damage. An embargo by the Organization of Petroleum Exporting Countries (OPEC) took place in fall 1973, shaking up American drivers and making them think about fuel economy more than ever before. Like the rest of Detroit, Chevrolet was slow to effectively respond to these and other sweeping changes in the marketplace. Still, despite the energy crisis and the growing demand for small cars, big Chevys sold well during this period and model-year production never went below 400,000.

Left: *Big Chevys got as big as they'd ever be with a 1971 redesign introducing rounded "fuselage" styling on a new 121.5-inch wheelbase. The Kingswood Estate topped the four-tier station wagon line.*

Left: *Full-size 1972 Chevys returned from their '71 makeover with a half-inch-longer wheelbase and minor styling changes. The most popular variant for '72 was the Impala four-door sedan, which went for $3708 with a 350-cubic-inch V-8.*

Right: *A Kingswood Estate wagon takes center stage in this '72 Chevy ad.* **Far right:** *The top-line Caprice became Caprice Classic for '73. The cheapest version was the $4064 four-door sedan. The vinyl roof (shown here) cost another $106.*

Right: *All big Chevys got a more squarish grille and more formal front end styling for 1974. Top-line Caprice Classic models, like this four-door sedan, wore a grille and inboard parking lights that were exclusive to the series.*

1981-1984

Right: *As before, Caprice Classics boasted exclusive styling touches and more upscale trim than their Impala siblings for 1982.* **Below:** *The '81 Caprice Classic was available with an economical but trouble-prone diesel V-8 engine.*

The massive "downsizing" that all of GM's full-size vehicles underwent for 1977 seemed like a risky gamble at the time, but by the early Eighties it was clear GM had made the right move. Chevrolet's Caprice Classic/Impala line fared as well as its corporate stablemates, gaining a crisp, squared-up body design that would serve it well for more than a decade. Of course, steady updates and improvements helped keep the basic shape fresh. Smaller, more economical powerplants reflected an increased focus on economy: A standard 3.8-liter V-6 and an ill-fated diesel V-8 option were both introduced for 1980. The long-serving Impala nameplate was retired after 1985.

Right: *The 1983 full-size Chevys saw little change, save for the expected grille-texture and trim updates. An improving national economy helped boost sales 17 percent to 220,795 this year.*

Right: *Unlike their sedan counterparts, big Chevy wagons came standard with V-8 power: a 150-hp 305. A heavy-duty suspension was a new option for 1984.*

1995

By 1995, the American automotive market was in the midst of a significant shift in buyer preferences. Traditional full-size sedans and station wagons were being pushed out of the mainstream by a new type of family hauler: the sport-utility vehicle, or SUV. Like other automakers, Chevrolet began shifting its new-product focus more to the SUV side of the spectrum, but didn't neglect its passenger cars entirely. An all-new Lumina sedan debuted for 1995 in base and upscale LS trim, and provided fresh competition for Ford's still-popular Taurus and other rivals. Meanwhile, the full-size Caprice Classic lineup, which had debuted for the 1991 model year, was nearing the end of its life. The entire Caprice line would disappear from Chevrolet's roster after 1996, as the company focused on the popular (and more profitable) SUV models. This marked the end of the rear-wheel-drive, body-on-frame family sedan at Chevrolet.

Right: *Woodgrain exterior trim was a $595 option on Caprice Classic wagons, which came standard with a healthy 260-hp 5.7-liter V-8. These big haulers were never great sellers; only 5030 were built for 1995.*

Left: *White Lumina sedans could get a monochromatic "Euro" look via white wheel covers, which were a no-cost option. Base Luminas started at $15,460 this year.*

2011 Volt

Right: *The Volt production prototype boasted a sleek, wind-cheating shape with high-tech styling details. If the Volt delivers on GM's promises, it could significantly change the American automotive landscape.*

First shown to the public in concept-car form at the 2007 North American International Auto Show, the hotly anticipated Chevrolet Volt was slated to go on sale as a 2011 production vehicle in late 2010. Though commonly referred to as a hybrid, the Volt differs from most hybrids in that its gasoline engine never powers the drive wheels. Rather, the gas engine only turns on to recharge Volt's lithium-ion batteries, which in turn power an electric motor. The batteries may also be recharged by plugging the car into a standard electrical outlet. GM claimed that Volt could drive up to 40 miles solely on battery power, and estimated a total driving range of 640 miles with assistance from the gas engine. Volt pricing was expected to be in the $40,000 range.

Right: *The pre-production Volt's futuristic-looking interior utilized plenty of glossy white plastic on the center console. GM stylists were likely inspired by the clean design of Apple computers and the popular iPod music players.*

Left: *Despite its extreme "green car" potential, the Volt retained a practical design with four-passenger capacity and a rear hatchback for cargo versatility.*

CHAPTER TWO

Sunshine Specials

Though the very first Chevrolets were all open-air vehicles, "true" convertible models—cars with fixed windshields, non-removable folding tops, and roll-up windows instead of snap-in side curtains—didn't join the roster until midyear 1928. By 1940, a convertible offering was a regular part of the Chevrolet model lineup. Like other automakers' ragtops, Chevy convertibles usually came only in the top-line "glamour" trim level of the year. Next to the station-wagon models, they were typically the most expensive offering in the lineup, and sold in limited numbers compared to their more practical siblings. America's love affair with full-size convertibles was sputtering by the early Seventies, but Chevrolet hung on longer than most...the last Caprice Classic ragtops appeared for 1975. Today, open-air fun in a new Chevrolet is offered only in the Corvette and soon-to-arrive Camaro ragtops.

This 1963 promotional photo showcases Chevrolet's small, medium, and large ragtops for the year: the Corvair Monza Spyder (top), Chevy II Nova (middle), and Impala (bottom).

1932 Confederate

Right: *The Landau Phaeton sold for $625 in base trim or $640 in DeLuxe trim, which added the twin trumpet horns, cowl lights, and chromed hood-vent doors seen here.*

Far left: *Landau Phaetons offered a small enclosed trunk that could be supplemented with an external luggage rack.* **Left:** *"Queen of the Shows" indeed! The Landau Phaeton looked especially handsome in profile.*

Sturdy, stylish, and brimming with value, the 1932 Chevrolets helped General Motors hold fast through the worst of the Great Depression. As the economic storm battered the company's higher-priced lines that year, Chevrolet would be the only GM division still making a profit. As was Chevy's custom at the time, the '32 models underwent another name change for the year, this time to Confederate. A more efficient downdraft carburetor boosted the sturdy "Stovebolt" six to 60 horsepower, a gain of 10, and a new "Silent Second Synchromesh" transmission virtually eliminated gear-grinding shifts. Despite the improvements, Chevy car sales dropped nearly 50 percent. One casualty of the dismal sales numbers was the Landau Phaeton, a unique "bustleback" convertible-sedan body style that had debuted just a year before. It attracted a mere 1602 customers for 1932, and thus did not return for 1933.

1941 Special DeLuxe

America was out of the Depression by 1941, largely due to increased military production prompted by an alarming new war in Europe. Industry heeded President Roosevelt's call to become an "arsenal of democracy," which all but eliminated unemployment but brought on inflation. Chevrolet proudly rolled out its 16-millionth vehicle, a Special DeLuxe Sport Sedan. Though clearly evolved from 1940, the '41 Chevys sported a more sharply raked windshield, in-fender headlamps, and a definite "big car" look overall. Indeed, many still regard the 1941 Chevy as a sort of scaled-down Buick. Not surprisingly, the $949 convertible coupe remained the style leader; it was Chevrolet's lone drop-top offering, and it came only in top-line Special DeLuxe trim. Production hit 15,296.

Opposite: *Early Forties cars boasted plenty of wonderful art-deco details, and the '41 Chevys were no exception. Pictured here are the dazzling accessory hood ornament and jukebox-like radio control panel.*
Right: *This Special DeLuxe convertible coupe wears optional fog lamps, stainless-steel fender trim, bumper wing guards, and chrome wheel-trim rings.*

1946-1948

Above: *The postwar car business was definitely a seller's market. At $1628, the '47 Fleetmaster convertible's price was up a steep $152 from 1946.*

Right: *The first postwar Chevrolets started rolling off the assembly line on October 3, 1945. At $1476, the 1946 Fleetmaster convertible was one of the costliest Chevys.*

Left: *For 1948, Fleetmaster interiors again sported "woodgrain" paint on the top of the dash, plus a deluxe steering wheel with horn ring.* **Below:** *A 1948 Fleetmaster convertible was the first of what would be many Chevys to pace the Indianapolis 500.*

Above: *Starting in 1947, Chevy dealers could cash in on the fad for "woodie" convertibles by applying a Country Club kit. The wood framing and Di-Noc panels also fit coupes and Aerosedans.*

Like most Detroit makes after World War II, Chevrolet reprised its 1942 models for 1946 with minor appearance changes. Three series continued, but Master DeLuxe was retitled Stylemaster and Special DeLuxe was now Fleetmaster. Despite huge pent-up demand for all cars, Chevrolet struggled against shortages of certain materials and a crippling strike that hit all of General Motors just as civilian production resumed, resulting in artificially low output for both the 1946 calendar and model years. Production got back up to speed for '47, rising to a healthy 671,543 units despite only minor styling tweaks such as a new grille and revised trim. The 1948 Chevys again saw only minimal changes, such as the addition of a vertical "T" grille bar. That would change for 1949, however, when completely redesigned Chevys debuted.

1953-1954

Right: *The Bel Air convertible was the most dashing of all '53 Chevrolets; its most daring styling element was the two-toning on the rear fenders, which was reserved for Bel Airs only.*

Left: *Chevrolet executives marked production of the 30-millionth Chevrolet, a new Bel Air convertible, on June 9, 1954.*

In addition to their fresh styling, the 1953 Chevys got new series names and a standard 235.5-cubic-inch six-cylinder engine. The "Blue Flame" six was previously limited to Powerglide cars, though the latter had slightly higher compression for 115 horsepower versus 108 with the stickshift. Power steering joined the options list this year, though its rather stiff $178 tariff kept demand relatively low. For 1954, more comfort and convenience options followed: power brakes ($38), power front windows ($86), and a power front seat (also $86). These "Stovebolt" Chevys sold well, but company executives realized that the brand's image was becoming a bit stale and needed an injection of youthful vigor. The all-new '55s would take care of that.

Below: *There were relatively few rear-end changes in Chevy's 1954 facelift, though bumper and taillights were revised.* **Right:** *Output of the $2185 Bel Air convertible slipped to 19,383 units for '54. This example wears accessory front bumper guards.*

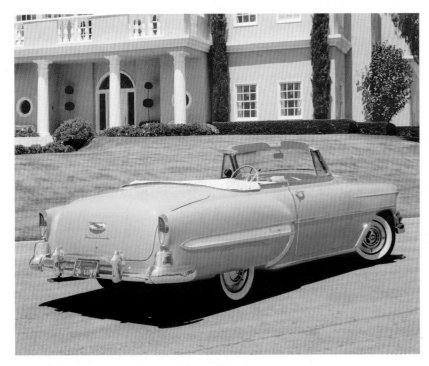

1955-1957

Above: *This ad depicts a 1955 Bel Air convertible at one of the first* Pebble Beach *Concours d'Elegance classic-car competitions in California—an accurate prediction of the '55 Chevy's high collectible status today.* **Middle:** *Bel Air ragtops offered handsome two-tone interiors and soft tops in beige, green, blue, or white.*
Below right:
A Bel Air convertible paced the Indianapolis 500 on May 30, 1955.

Left and below: *The Bel Air convertible remained queen of the Chevy line for '55, priced at $2206 to start. A power top and electric window lifts were among the many factory options.*

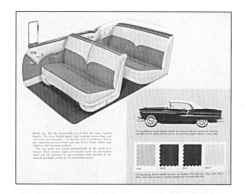

Right: *This India Ivory/ Sherwood Green '56 Bel Air convertible sports optional wire wheel covers.* **Far right:** *For 1957, Chevy convertible sales set a new record at 47,562 units. Still, that amounted to only 6.8 percent of the 702,220 total Bel Airs built for the model year.* **Below:** *The '57 Bel Airs wore an exclusive brushed-aluminum panel in their bodyside trim.*

Rightly advertised as "The Hot One," the car with "New Look! New Life! New Everything!," the 1955 Chevy would change the company's image forever. No longer the staid, stodgy, "old man's car" of yore, Chevrolet now offered sleek "Motoramic" styling, "V-8 engineering," and hot performance. For 1956, ads proclaimed "The Hot One's Even Hotter!," and indeed it was. Chevrolet engineering wizard Zora Arkus-Duntov set an American Stock Sedan record in the grueling Pikes Peak Hill Climb in a prototype 1956 Chevy. Another iconic facelift and still more horsepower debuted for '57. Given their celebrated status now, it's easy to forget that the '57 Chevys actually came in second to archrival Ford in that year's sales race.

1958 Impala

This page: *One of several new nameplates at Chevy for 1958, the lush top-line Impala naturally got pride of place in most of that year's ads.*

YOU'LL GET A REAL CHARGE *out of the way this* **'58 CHEVROLET** *responds to your touch, the slightest hint of command. Here's vigorous new V8 performance that's enough to perk up anybody's pride. Here's quick, eager-to-please handling that lets you know you're the boss, right from the start!*

That's a wonderful feeling, you know. But it doesn't happen by chance; it's a careful blend of qualities that demands real engineering talent.

Very few cars in any price range even come close to Chevy's precise, clean ease of handling, the beautifully balanced way it clings to any road, the crisp accuracy of its steering, the supple sure-footedness of its Full Coil suspension.

There's never been another list of tremendous advances like the '58

Chevrolet's Level Air 100 percent air springs*, its low-slung X-built frame, its unprecedented Turbo-Thrust V8 engines*, its totally new bodies. But the biggest advance in the new Chevrolet is the whole new feeling of ease and competence and security. You won't know how significant *that* is till you try it—and that's something you ought to do this week! . . . *Chevrolet Division of General Motors, Detroit 2, Michigan.* *Optional at extra cost.

CHEVROLET

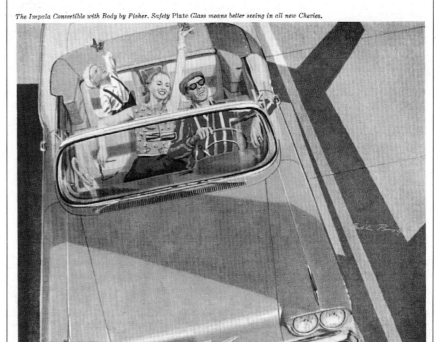

The Impala Convertible with Body by Fisher. Safety Plate Glass means better seeing in all new Chevies.

YOU'LL HAVE PLENTY TO SHOW OFF *in the high-spirited performance of your* **NEW CHEVROLET.** *With its radical new Turbo-Thrust V8* and new action in all engines, it's so quick, agile and eager that once you take the wheel, you'll never want to leave it. You've got your hands on something really special!*

Your pride can't help showing just a bit when you slide behind the wheel of this new Chevrolet. You couldn't be sitting prettier—and you know it.

You're in charge of one of the year's most looked at, most longed for cars. Chevy's crisply sculptured contours and downright luxurious interiors are enough to make anybody feel like a celebrity.

Move your foot a fraction on the gas pedal and you feel the instant, silken response of a unique new kind of V8. You ride smoothly and serenely—cushioned by deep coil springs at every wheel. You can even have a real air ride*, if you wish.

See your Chevrolet dealer. . . . Chevrolet Division of General Motors, Detroit 2, Mich. *Optional at extra cost.

CHEVROLET

Chevrolet's eye-opening 1958 cars were bigger, heavier, cushier, and more powerful than before. Wheelbase stretched out to 117.5 inches on an all-new X-frame chassis that adopted rear coil springs—or the option of four-wheel air suspension. "Sculpturamic" styling featured quad headlights, "jet-intake" parking lights, and canted rear fenders. The Bel Air added a flashy subseries, a hardtop coupe and convertible with a name destined for greatness: Impala. Detroit's 1950s styling race was reaching its peak by the end of the decade. All 1958 GM cars were encrusted with elaborate chrome trim, but the Chevrolets seemed to wear it better than their corporate stablemates.

Right: *A broad hood "V" again denoted a V-8 under '58 Chevy hoods, and most Impalas were so equipped. The new 348-cubic-inch option was a good match for the heavier '58 models.*

1959-1960 Impala

Right: *Even with the top up, a 1959 Impala convertible cuts a dazzling profile. Impala grew into a full series including a sedan and hardtop sedan body style, and ended up being the most popular trim level for the year.*

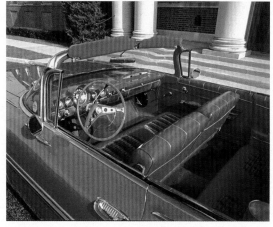

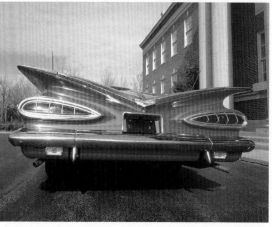

Far left: *Interiors gained nearly five inches in width, plus a bulkier new-design dashboard.*
Left: *Trunks were bigger than ever for '59 at 32 cubic feet, but rather tough to reach due to the outlandish styling.*

Right: *One could hardly call a 1960 Impala convertible "subdued," though styling was toned down a bit from '59. Convertibles cost $2954 with base V-8 and garnered 79,903 total sales.*

Created amid a "crash program" response to Chrysler Corporation's trend-setting 1957 cars, the wild new 1959 Chevys were far-out even by the free-wheeling standards of the time. Engines were much the same as in '58, ranging from the stalwart 235.5-cubic-inch six to 283- and 348-cube V-8s. The '59 Chevys sold well, but the company realized it might have gone a bit too far with the over-the-top design. Chevy's 1960 big-car styling softened the '59 rear-end look with reshaped and separated "bat wing" tailfins, plus orthodox round taillamps. Recontoured rear fenders adopted aircraft inspired chrome trim, as Chevy began emphasizing "jet smoothness." Powerplants were basically carried over from '59. It was a neck-and-neck sales race between Ford and Chevy for 1959, but Chevy pulled far ahead for 1960, outpacing Ford by nearly half a million units. The 1960 models would end up being the last of the true tailfinned Chevys, and a fitting end to an era.

1964-1967 Chevelle

Right: *The new Chevelle essentially matched the overall size and proportions of the classic '55 "shoebox" Chevys.*
Below: *This Malibu convertible shows off the clean, handsome lines that distinguished every new '64 Chevelle.*

STYLING THAT MOVES YOU EVEN WHEN IT'S STANDING STILL

By the early Sixties, Detroit's mainline passenger cars had grown into truly hefty machines. Between these so-called standards and the recently introduced compacts, there was room for another class of car: the intermediate. General Motors plunged into this new market in a big way in 1964, pumping up the existing compacts from Pontiac, Oldsmobile, and Buick and introducing the Chevrolet Chevelle. The new midsize Chevys were up to 16 inches shorter than their full-sized companions and up to 3.5 inches narrower. After a handsome facelift for 1965, the Chevelle line got swoopier curves via a 1966 reskin, and another deft facelift for '67. As expected, convertibles were the flagships of the line.

Above: *Chevelle got the usual second-year cosmetic changes for '65. This Malibu was one of 19,765 Chevelle ragtops built that model year.*

Right: *Sporty SS models became SS 396 models for 1966, with the addition of a standard 396-cubic-inch "big block" V-8. Convertibles started at $2964. This example wears the base small hubcaps, but redline tires add some pizzazz.*

Above: *This $3033 ragtop was one of 63,000 SS Chevelles built for the 1967 model year. Though that was down a bit from the '66 tally, the "muscle" era was nevertheless in full swing.*

1965-1968 Impala

Right: *"Evening Orchid" was the name of one of Chevy's most distinctive color choices for 1965, and it looked great on the Impala SS convertible. The wide-whitewall tires seen on this example are an aftermarket addition.*

Chevy's full-size cars were completely new for 1965, starting with a perimeter frame with wider front and rear tracks, and topped by sleek new styling. After a crisp facelift for '66, all-new bodies debuted for '67 with swoopy "coke bottle" curves. The '68s were mildly refreshed with slightly inset headlight "pods" and other styling updates. Debuting in mid-1965 to replace the beloved 409 was an all-new "big-block" 396-cid V-8. For 1967, an even-burlier 427-cube version was added.

Left: *Super Sport Impalas came standard with a buckets-and-console interior, and shared a new dashboard design with other big Chevys.*

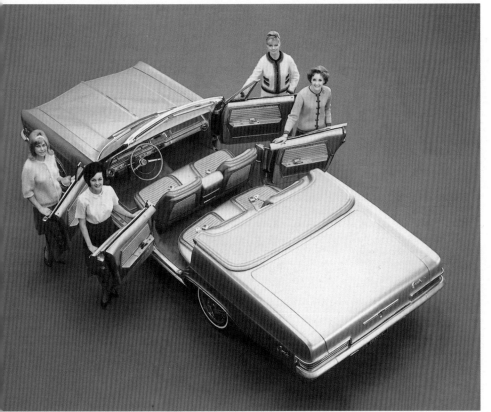

Above: *Chevrolet never actually produced a four-door convertible in the Sixties, but did try out the concept on this intriguing show car: the 1966 Caribe.*
Above right: *Though the Caprice name ousted Impala as Chevy's top-line full-size car for '66, ragtops still came only as Impalas.*

Above: *The '67 Impala convertible started at $3254 with standard V-8 and saw 9545 copies. Swoopy body curves are evident in this side-profile view.* **Left:** *By 1968, sporty big cars were clearly overshadowed by their little-brother intermediate kin. Chevrolet still offered the Impala Super Sport, but as a $179 option package instead of a separate model lineup.*

1974-1975 Caprice

This page: *In addition to new front-end styling, all 1974 big Chevys got a rear end reprofiled to accept a newly required 5-mph bumper. Caprice Classic ragtops started at $4745 this year.*

Right: *The 1975 Caprice Classics wore a more streamlined nose and fresher taillights than their Impala counterparts, which made do with slightly altered 1974 styling.*

Despite their fun-in-the-sun nature, convertibles had always been relatively weak sellers due to their high prices, rattle-prone bodies, and lack of all-weather practicality. By the early Seventies, traditional full-size convertibles were truly on the ropes. The Caprice Classic was no exception, with 1974 sales tumbling from 7339 units to just 4670. Chevrolet persisted for one more year, building 8349 "last-hurrah" 1975 Caprice Classic ragtops before exiting the full-size convertible market.

Left: *The '75 Caprice Classic convertible started at $5113, but speculators and nostalgia buffs drove actual transaction prices much higher.*

1984-2000 Cavalier

Left: *For 1986, the Type 10 option was replaced by even sportier RS trim. Included were wider tires, sport suspension, red and black exterior accents, and special interior.*
Bottom: *The Cavalier RS convertible remained pretty rare in 1987 with just 5826 sales. A new "Generation II" 2.0-liter four upped base horsepower to 90, and a similarly updated Gen II V-6 delivered 125 at extra cost.*

Above: *Cavaliers were freshened up for '84 with quad rectangular headlights and a tidy eggcrate grille. Convertibles started at $11,299 and came only in sporty Type 10 trim.*

Right: *For 1988, the topline Cavalier Z24 was made available in convertible as well as coupe form. Swoopy "ground effects" body-side sills and unique aluminum wheels were part of the Z24 package.* **Far right:** *Both Z24 and RS (shown) ragtops got a glass rear window for 1993, which improved rear visibility with the top up.* **Bottom:** *The swan-song Cavalier convertible appeared for the 2000 model year, and was available only in Z24 trim. Sadly, the new-for-2005 Cobalt compact did not include a convertible body style.*

Though the 1975 Caprice Classic was purported to be the "last" Chevy ragtop, it would be less than a decade before a convertible rejoined Chevrolet's model lineup. The compact Cavalier joined Chevy's lineup for 1982, and a ragtop variant was added in '83. In 1988, Cavaliers got new lower body sheetmetal, but mechanical changes were few. The basic Cavalier platform served until 1995, when an all-new models with sleeker styling debuted. Cavalier convertibles were discontinued for good after the 2000 model year; the coupes and sedans soldiered on until 2005, after which they were phased out by the all-new Cobalt.

CHAPTER THREE

Glamour Queens

General Motors pioneered the mass-produced "hardtop convertible" body style with all-new 1949 Buick Roadmaster Riviera, Cadillac Series 62 Coupe de Ville, and Oldsmobile 98 Holiday. Although they arrived late in the model year, all three were such outstanding commercial successes that every other U.S. automaker scrambled to catch up. Chevrolet got its own high-fashion hardtop in the 1950 Bel Air, and it too was a sales hit from the start. Along with "jet-age" tailfins (another GM styling innovation), swoopy pillarless-hardtop bodystyles were key weapons in the styling race of the Fifties. By the mid-Seventies, however, changing buyer tastes and the spectre of increased rollover safety regulations conspired to bring the hardtop era to an end. Chevrolet produced its last true hardtop models for 1976.

By the mid-Fifties, automotive glamour was more important than ever. Even buyers of low-priced cars were concerned with "keeping up with the Joneses," as this 1955 Bel Air hardtop ad reveals.

How to look your best when everybody's looking

Who says a picture isn't worth a thousand words?

Here's one that shows you what's going on in all kinds of places where young people gather today . . . when a new Motoramic Chevrolet puts in an appearance.

This car's so perky it looks like it's always going to a party! And they love it because it represents *them* . . . because it's young and fresh and eager in style and power and performance.

And if you nudge the pedal when the light goes green . . . you'll find nothing ahead of you but fresh air. And when you make a turn you'll find it corners like a sports car. *Blithe spirit!*

That new V8 engine acts as if you'd told the engineers what to make it do! And those two new and powerful 6's will give you more power than you'll ever want to use.

This car's got a lot to offer in the power-feature department, too. Braking, steering, gear shifting — even seat and window adjustments too, on Bel Air and "Two-Ten" models — all these little motoring chores can be done the "pushbutton" way in the Motoramic Chevrolet through extra-cost options.

So, drop around one of these fine days and get set to look *your* best when everybody's looking.

SEE YOUR CHEVROLET DEALER

motoramic

Stealing the thunder from the high-priced cars!

1950-1952 Bel Air

Above and right: *A simplified grille and a new hood ornament were among the few styling changes that set the 1950 Chevrolets apart from their immediate predecessors.*

Left: *Bel Air hardtops were available only in the top-end Styleline DeLuxe trim level, which included a flashier, two-tone interior treatment.*
Above: *Powerglide-equipped Chevys wore extra trim announcing that fact on the trunk handle.*

Right and below:
Chevy cars again saw only minor trim changes for 1951. Reflecting strong postwar inflation, the price of a Bel Air hardtop rose to $1914, a one-year jump of $173, which in those days was a significant increase.

As if Powerglide automatic transmission wasn't enough, Chevrolet had another trump card for 1950 in America's first low-priced pillarless coupe: the new Styleline DeLuxe Bel Air. Like the senior GM "hardtop convertibles" introduced the previous year, it appealed for combining the comfort of a closed car with the open-air sportiness of a true convertible. Chevy even used convertible-type frame reinforcing to make up for the missing center roof post. Besides the new transmission and body style, the '50

Chevys were little changed. Even so, production and sales set new records during 1950, partly because the Korean conflict sparked fears that Detroit might shut down civilian production, as it had in 1942. Though that didn't happen, the U.S. government did divert some strategic materials from civilian to military production, which limited automobile production somewhat in '51 and '52. The Bel Air continued to be a strong seller, however, and Ford and Plymouth joined the fray for '51. The hardtop era was officially underway.

Above: *The '52 Chevys were very mildly face-lifted via a "toothier" grille and minor trim shuffles. The Bel Air now had strong competition from Plymouth's Cranbrook Belvedere hardtop and Ford's fully-redesigned Victoria.*

1955 Bel Air

Right: *The 1955 Bel Air sport coupe looked great from any angle. Press releases called it "an excellent example of smart profile styling." Buyers must have agreed; more than 185,000 of these hardtops were built.*

Opposite right: *In the mid-Fifties, the autumn unveiling of an auto manufacturer's new model lineup was a major media event. Shown here is the "press kit" for Chevy's 1955 cars.* **Opposite far right:** *Developed in just 15 weeks, Chevy's new 265-cid V-8 was the most revolutionary of the changes for '55. It was the company's first V-8 since its poor-selling attempt of 1917–18, and it quickly became the standard for modern Detroit performance.*

Right: *The breezy, open-air look of the hardtop body style is clearly illustrated in this Bel Air sport coupe ad.* **Far right:** *On November 23, 1954, a '55 Chevy Bel Air sport coupe rolled down the Flint, Michigan, assembly line as General Motors' 50-millionth car. In addition to Anniversary Gold paint, this milestone vehicle wore 716 gold-plated trim parts.*

Aside from its fresh, dazzling styling, the 1955 Chevrolet's biggest news was its all-new V-8 engine. Designed by veteran GM engineers Harry Barr and Ed Cole, this new "Turbo-Fire" engine pioneered an innovative block-casting technique that made for uncommon manufacturing precision, especially in the low-priced field. With the standard two-barrel carburetor, the efficient Turbo-Fire offered 162 lively horses from 265 cubic inches and a mild 8.0:1 compression ratio. Available dual exhausts and four-barrel carb boosted horsepower to 180, and a racing-oriented 195-hp setup was added late in the model year. Despite its superior horsepower output, the new V-8 ended up weighing 40 pounds less than Chevy's familiar "Blue Flame" six-cylinder powerplant. The Turbo-Fire transformed Chevy's image from dull family car to a dynamic performer that ads appropriately termed "The Hot One."

1956-1957 Bel Air

Right: *Chevy had some of the slickest two-tone treatments around, as this Onyx Black/Crocus Yellow Bel Air sport coupe illustrates.*

Right and below: *GM pioneered four-door hardtops in 1955 at Buick and Oldsmobile. For '56, Chevy joined in by adding a pillarless sport sedan to its top-line Bel Air and middle-range Two-Ten series.*

Right and below:
If any car defines the Fifties, it has to be the amply facelifted 1957 Chevy. Chevrolet issued 166,426 Bel Air sport coupes, typically loaded with extra-cost goodies.
Far right: *Four-door hardtops returned for '57 in both Two-Ten (shown) and Bel Air trim.*

Chevrolet stepped up its hardtop game for 1956 by adding a slick four-door hardtop sedan to the model lineup. Performance was stepped up too, with a livelier new "Super Turbo-Fire" V-8 packing 205 horsepower with four-barrel carburetor and 9.25:1 compression ratio—Chevy's highest yet. A linewide option, it was joined at midyear by a 225-hp twin-four-barrel version

lifted from the all-new '56 Corvette. Even more horsepower was on tap for '57 with the addition of an enlarged 283-cubic-inch V-8. The new 283 was available in six versions ranging from 185 to 283 horsepower via two-barrel, four-barrel, and twin-four-barrel carburetor setups, plus the new Ramjet fuel injection. The veteran "Blue Flame Six" was still available as well.

1958

The larger, softer-riding '58 Chevys lost some of the edge their predecessors had in motorsports events, but still could deliver healthy performance when equipped with the new 348-cubic-inch V-8. The regular four-barrel "Turbo Thrust" version made 250 horsepower, while the "Super Turbo-Thrust" delivered 280 horses with triple two-barrel carbs or 315 with high-compression heads and solid lifters. A recession hit the U.S. economy just as 1958 models hit showrooms, and Chevrolet suffered like most other Detroit makes. Model-year production slid to just over 1.1 million, down 363,450 units from '57. Even so, Chevy reclaimed its rank as "USA-1," besting archrival Ford by some 154,500 cars. Volume would go even higher for '59.

Below: *Impala's '58 sales were good, all things considered: about 125,000 hardtops and 56,000 convertibles.*

Above: *A 1958 Impala hardtop is shown here fronting that year's newly restyled Corvette. At the top is the Biscayne show car from the '55 GM Motorama; to the right, the sleek '57 Corvette Sebring SS racer.* **Right:** *An Impala hardtop was featured on the cover of Chevy's 1958 accessories catalog.*

Right: *Dummy rear-fender scoops, triple taillights, and a faux rear roof scoop were just a few of the Impala's exclusive styling features.*
Far right: *For buyers who wanted to give their Impala even more glitz, Chevrolet offered a plethora of dealer accessories, including a continental spare tire kit, twin aerial antennas, and fake rear-fender "exhaust ports."*

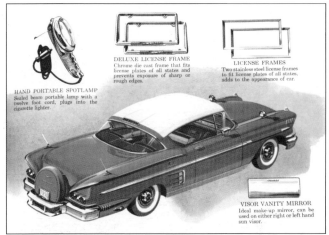

Left: *The Bel Air hardtop coupe provided pillarless hardtop styling at a starting price of $2447—$139 less than an Impala.* **Above:** *Four-door hardtops came only in Bel Air trim, and started at $2511 with a six or $2618 with a V-8.*

1959-1960 Impala

This page: *Chevy's new 1959 passenger cars, such as this Impala sport coupe, generated big controversy with their "batwing" fins, "cat's eye" taillights, and a rear deck "big enough to land a Piper Cub," as one journalist wrote.*

Impala became a separate series for 1959, adding four-door hardtop and four-door sedan body styles to the existing two-door sport coupe and convertible. Sport coupes featured a shortened roofline and wrap-over back window, promising a "virtually unlimited rear view" to complement the car's new compound-curve windshield. The hardtop sport sedan had a huge, pillar-free back window, allowing for scads of headroom beneath its slender "flying wing" roofline. Styling was toned down for 1960 as GM designers sensed a move away from the flamboyant excess of the Fifties, but flashy Impala models still easily outsold the plainer Bel Airs and Biscaynes.

Right: *Chevy's 1960 four-door hardtops wore a unique "flat-top" roofline with a wraparound rear window, a design carried over from 1959. Impalas like this one started at $2662 with six-cylinder power.*

Left: *Flashy, exuberant color choices were much more important in the Fifties and Sixties than they are today. Pictured here are Chevrolet's offerings for 1960.*

Left: *The '60 Chevys revived the round-taillamp motif of 1958. Impalas like this sport coupe got six; Bel Airs and Biscaynes made do with four.*

1961-1963 Impala

Right and far right: *Four-door hardtops got a formal new roofline with much thicker rear-roof pillars for 1961. Impalas like these started at $2769 with the base 283-cubic-inch V-8.*

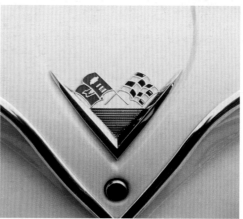

Left: *Two-door hardtops like this Impala wore a wispy "bubbletop" roofline. Note the faux vents beneath the rear window and the way the trunklid emblem neatly slots into the stamped body character line.*

Right: *Along with the cleaned-up, squared-off restyle that all big Chevys received for 1962, the Impala sport coupe received a new roof design. In place of the bubbletop was a more-formal hardtop with a ribbed rear roofline and smaller back window to mimic the look of a cloth convertible top.*

Above and left: *With 195 horsepower, Chevy's base 283 V-8 was 25 hp stronger for '63. So equipped, an Impala Sport Coupe listed at $2774. Smart new bodywork included a crisp rear deck above a newly concave taillight panel.*

Chevrolet was on a roll in the early Sixties, and the flashy-yet-classy Impalas were leading the way. Astonishing sales increases were achieved every model year as the Impala line continued to handily outsell its downmarket siblings. Impala production totaled around 491,000 cars for '61, 704,900 for '62, and 832,600 for '63. In 1962, Impalas accounted for nearly 52 percent of full-size Chevrolet volume, outselling the nearest competitive line—Ford's Galaxie—by nearly two to one. Chevrolet's unmatched dealer body contributed greatly to this success, of course, and the factory sales organization pushed relentlessly not only to retain leadership, but to gain an even greater lead.

1965-1966

This page: *Impala SS sport coupes saw a healthy production run of around 222,000 units for 1965. V-8s easily out-sold six-cylinder versions, no surprise in those days of cheap gas and afford-able horsepower.*

It's called Caprice. It's made by Chevrolet. It's built to compare with any other elegant car.

Caprice
CHEVROLET

This page: *Caprice two-door hardtops wore a more formal roofline than their Impala kin. All of Chevy's full-size '66 cars received subtle styling changes: Fenders, bumpers, and grille were new, and taillights were now wraparound on upper-series models.*

Big Chevy bodies managed to grow bigger still for 1965, featuring dramatically rounded sides, curved window glass, and an all-new front end with fresh hood contours. Just as Impala had supplanted Bel Air as Chevy's top trim level, so too would Impala be dethroned by a new premium offering: Caprice. Chevrolet added a $200 Caprice option for the Impala four-door hardtop at mid '65. Included were a lush interior, special trim, and a heavy-duty frame. For 1966, Caprice became a full-fledged model line offering station-wagon and two- and four-door hardtop body styles. All featured unique styling touches outside and opulent interiors with simulated woodgrain trim. With its upper-class appointments and friendly Chevy prices, Caprice was a strong seller for '66, attracting some 181,000 value-wise shoppers.

1967-1970

Right: *A major restyle gave 1967 full-size Chevrolets an artful blend of creases, bulges, and curves. Even mainline Impalas like this one could be equipped with the top engine option: a stout 385-hp 427 V-8.* **Middle:** *The arcing two-door hardtop roof used on many 1965–66 General Motors cars was extended to near-fastback proportions for 1967.* **Bottom:** *Fender skirts and vertical front corner lamps were options on the Impala.*

Below: *All other big Chevys were available with a choice of six- or eight-cylinder power, but plush Caprices came only with V-8s. The Caprice four-door hardtop started at $3078.*

MAKES ELEGANCE AN EVERYDAY AFFAIR

The 1967 Caprice Custom Sedan. Elegance begins with Body by Fisher, of course.

Every year one or two cars stand conspicuously apart. Like '67 Caprice by Chevrolet.

It's a unique car that offers elegance you want at a price most new-car buyers desire.

THE GRAND CHEVROLET
'67 CAPRICE

Right: *Caprice sales came on strong for '68, as increasing numbers of Chevy shoppers were lured by the model's claims to luxury and status. Hardtop coupes started at $3219.*

The only American car
that gives you all these features at a popular price.

Caprice
The Grand Chevrolet

ull-size Chevrolets continued their evolutionary march through the latter half of the Sixties, with classy styling updates and new technological advancements every year. A Delco eight-track stereo was a new option for 1967. For '68, a raised lip at the trailing edge of the hood concealed new "Hide-Away" wipers—and eliminated the traditional cowl filler panel. Government-mandated front-shoulder safety belts became standard on cars built after January 1, 1968. A seldom-ordered '69 option was the "Liquid Tire Chain Dispensing System." It sprayed the rear tires with a traction-enhancing chemical when more grip was needed on frozen surfaces. A headlamps-on warning/timed-delay-off system and stalk-mounted wiper controls were handy new extras for the 1970 models.

Above and middle: *Redesigning for 1969 gave the big Chevrolets a sculptured look on their bodysides and a slightly longer appearance overall. This Impala sport coupe has the rare 427 V-8 and a four-speed manual transmission.* **Bottom:** *Another restyle and an optional 454-cid V-8 made news for 1970. Shown here is the $3474 Caprice hardtop coupe.*

1971-1976

Above and middle: *The redesigned 1971 full-size Chevys had a "junior Cadillac" look about them that no doubt helped sales; total output hit 764,943. Pictured here is the $3826 Impala Custom coupe.*

New Caprice. The most distinguished Chevrolet of all.

1973 Chevrolet. Building a better way to see the U.S.A. Chevrolet

Left and bottom: *In 1973, Chevrolet's luxury leader had its best year ever to that point. Orders for the Caprice Classic totaled 275,258 cars, including 70,155 hardtop sedans and 77,134 hardtop coupes.*

Above: *Caprice Classics featured "stepped-back" headlamp bezels for '75. The hardtop sedan was the most popular Caprice that year, with a production run of 40,482.*

Left and below: *True pillarless-hardtop coupe styling disappeared from the Caprice Classic lineup for 1974, when a new "colonnade" roof with fixed quarter windows debuted. The 1976 Caprice Classics (shown here) weren't drastically changed from 1975, but did adopt new rectangular headlights.*

Over the years, Chevrolet had addressed changing trends in buyer tastes by expanding its lineup with new models that targeted specific buyer segments. In the Fifties, Chevy's mainstream passenger cars were built on one basic platform that hosted multiple body styles. By 1971, the roster included the subcompact Vega, compact Nova, midsize Chevelle/Chevelle wagon, sporty Camaro, and the personal-luxury Monte Carlo—all distinct model lineups built on various platforms. Chevy's full-size cars grew into even-bigger cruisers for '71, but a fuel crisis and the ensuing concerns about efficiency caused a sea change in the American auto market. As it turned out, the '71-'76s would be the last Chevrolets to continue the tradition of full-sized cars getting bigger and more opulent every year; radically downsized Caprices and Impalas appeared for '77.

CHAPTER FOUR

Budget Beauties

Chevrolet's forays into the small-car marketplace may not have been as consistently successful as the company's other ventures, but the history of Chevy compacts is no less colorful. Along with other major American automakers, Chevrolet focused primarily on a single lineup of "one-size-fits-all" cars for the first half of the 20th century. Those mainstream American cars kept growing larger and larger, until a recession in 1958 made America rethink "bigger is better." Then, with the rising tide of economical imports and a few successful American compact cars, Chevrolet couldn't ignore the small-car market any longer. Chevy introduced its first compact, the Corvair, in 1960. The Middle East oil embargo of 1973 and subsequent spikes in the price of fuel meant that small cars would hold a permanent position in the Chevrolet lineup.

The mid-line Corvair 700 coupe cost $1985 in 1961. Corvair, along with competitors Ford Falcon and Plymouth Valiant, debuted in 1960. The rear-engined Corvair was the most radical of the three.

1960-1969 Corvair

Right: *A full-perimeter chrome strip identified top-line Corvair 700 models like this sedan, which carried a starting price of $2103 in 1960.* **Far right:** *Chevy charged $2049 for this Corvair 700 club coupe, $1984 for the 500 version. Model year 1960 sales totaled just over 250,000, which looked good except against Ford's conventional new Falcon, which scored a smashing 435,000 that same season.*

1. Corvair Monza Club Coupe

2. Corvair Lakewood 500 Station Wagon

3. Corvair 500 4-Door Sedan

Three thrifty ways to go wandering

Well, who wouldn't like to get away from it all in cars like Corvair? Especially when it costs you so little. (Corvair's not only priced 'way down, every model keeps right on saving with quicker cold-start warmup, no antifreeze-buying blues, and lots of other ways your dealer will tell you about.) What's more, Corvair gives you your money's worth of riding comfort and handling ease. Make the first leg of your vacation trip a jaunt to your Chevrolet dealer's. Bon voyage! . . . Chevrolet Division of General Motors, Detroit 2, Michigan.

1. *Monza* — Wouldn't you look dashing, driving a Monza Club Coupe with its handsome bucket-type front seats!

2. *Lakewood* — Corvair's rear-engined station wagon gives you up to 68 cubic feet of space, 10 of it under that lockable bonnet.

3. *500 4-Door Sedan* — Nearly 12% more luggage space up front this year, but no change in Corvair's brisk handling.

'61 CHEVY CORVAIR corvair

Right: *Corvairs got more versatile for 1961 with the addition of a station wagon body style.* **Far right:** *Corvair wagons weren't great sellers, however. Only 2362 '62 Corvair Monza Lakewood wagons were built, and the body style was dropped for 1963.*

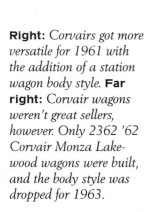

Right: *With the '65 restyle, all Corvair coupes and sedans were pillarless hardtops. The base engine developed 95 hp, and a turbocharged 180-hp engine was optional on the top-line Corsa models. The Monza coupe (shown) started at $2347.*

Left: *The '66 Corvair 500 sedan cost a reasonable $2157. Only 8779 were sold.* **Below:** *The second-generation Corvair received only minor changes until the line was dropped in 1969. Shown here is the $2522 Monza coupe.*

Chevrolet Division manager Edward Cole wanted to take on the leading import of the late Fifties—the Volkswagen Beetle—so he backed a design with an air-cooled engine in the rear, VW's signature feature. The resulting Corvair had an aluminum-block six that displaced 140 cubic inches and made 80 horsepower. Sporty Monza and Corsa series were available with a 150/180-hp turbocharged engine. The 108-inch-wheelbase unit-body Corvair was larger than most European compacts, but was quite small by American standards of the time. The rear suspension utilized independent swing axles that could cause tricky handling during fast cornering. That trait was publicized in Ralph Nader's book *Unsafe at Any Speed*. A redesigned Corvair appeared in '65 with sleeker lines and an improved independent rear suspension that tamed the handling problem, but by then the car's fate was sealed. Chevrolet shifted its focus to more-conventional, more-profitable vehicles, and the Corvair was gone by the end of the decade.

1962-1979 Chevy II/Nova

Right: *The Chevy II sold a healthy 327,000-some units in debut 1962, but it still couldn't beat Ford's still-popular Falcon. Here, the mid-line 300-series two-door sedan, priced from $2084.*

Above: *The sporty 1965 Chevy II Nova SS hardtop coupe could be had with V-8s up to 300 hp.* **Left and far left:** *The '66 Chevy II Nova SS Sport Coupe sold some 23,000 copies, nearly three-quarters of which were V-8 powered. Bucket seats were standard in SS models.*

Left: *The 1967 Chevy II Nova wagon listed at $2566 with the six, $2671 with V-8. The latter was seldom ordered in these compact haulers.*

Far left: *The redesigned '68 Nova was available only as two-door coupe or four-door sedan.* **Left:** *The 1970 Nova engines ranged from a 90-hp four to a 375-hp V-8. A Nova Custom Coupe is shown.* **Middle:** *Topping the 1975 Nova line was the LN (Luxury Nova) sedan.* **Bottom:** *The 1979 model year was a very short one for Nova, with production actually ending in November 1978. In spring of '79, it was replaced by the new front-wheel-drive Citation, introduced as an early 1980 model.*

Chevrolet quickly realized that the unconventional Corvair would never be as popular as the rival Ford Falcon. The answer, they thought, was a more mainstream small car. Just 18 months after the start of design work, the Chevy II came out as a 1962 model. A 153-cid four—Chevy's first since 1928—or a 194-cid six went underhood. In '64, a V-8 joined the range. Chevy II grew to almost intermediate size with a full redesign in 1968. Nova was initially the name of the top-line models, but in '69 the Chevy II name was retired in favor of Nova. A complete restyle for 1975 brought more-angular styling and increased glass area for better visibility. Nova carried on with minor changes through '79.

1971-1976 Vega

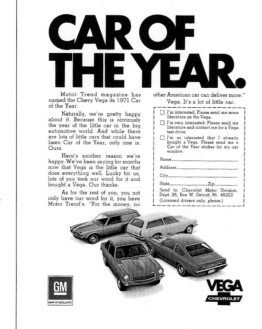

Right: *Vega was fun to drive and off to a good start, winning* Motor Trend's *Car of the Year award for '71. Troubles were soon to follow, however.* **Below:** *Anticipating America's Bicentennial, Vega's '74 "Spirit of America" package was eye-catching.* **Bottom:** *The rare 1975-76 Cosworth-Vegas aimed for European flair with an exotic 2.0-liter twin-cam four-cylinder. White was a '76-only color choice.*

CAR OF THE YEAR.

Motor Trend magazine has named the Chevy Vega its 1971 Car of the Year.

Naturally, we're pretty happy about it. Because this is obviously the year of the little car in the big automotive world. And while there are lots of little cars that could have been Car of the Year, only one is. Ours.

Here's another reason we're happy. We've been saying for months now that Vega is the little car that does everything well. Lucky for us, lots of you took our word for it and bought a Vega. Our thanks.

As for the rest of you, you not only have our word for it, you have Motor Trend's: "For the money, no other American car can deliver more." Vega. It's a lot of little car.

☐ I'm interested. Please send me some literature on the Vega.
☐ I'm very interested. Please send me literature and contact me for a Vega test-drive.
☐ I'm so interested that I already bought a Vega. Please send me a Car of the Year sticker for my car window.

Name_____
Address_____
City_____
State_____ Zip_____

Send to: Chevrolet Motor Division, Dept. 25, Box W, Detroit, Mi. 48202 (Licensed drivers only, please.)

GM MARK OF EXCELLENCE

VEGA CHEVROLET

Vega *seemed* like a good idea when it bowed for 1971. Riding a 97-inch wheelbase, the shortest in Chevy history, it carried an aluminum-block 140-cid overhead-camshaft four with 90 or 110 horsepower. Chevrolet spent vast sums designing its attempt to beat back the small imports. The Vega had many advanced—but unperfected—ideas in its engineering and manufacturing, and the car quickly became notorious for severe body rust and engine problems. Introduced in 1975, the sporty Monza shared the Vega's chassis. Monza also shared the Vega four and offered two small V-8s as well. By '78, both the Vega and its troublesome aluminum four were history. Monza carried on until 1980 with a new "Iron Duke" four-cylinder base engine.

Above: *The 1972 Vega Kammback wagon was priced from $2285 and attracted 71,957 orders. By now, Vega reliability woes were widespread; engines suffered from oil leaks and head warping, and bodies were subject to severe rust problems.*

1975-1980 Monza

Right: *The '75 Monza 2+2 hatchback coupe shared the Vega's chassis but offered nicer appointments, sportier looks, and optional V-8s with 110 or 125 hp.*

Far right, top: *Monza Towne Coupes wore more formal styling than their hatchback siblings. Shown here is the $3359 1976 model.*

Above: *The 1979 Monza 2+2 hatchback coupe's iron-block four put out 90 hp.* **Left:** *This 1980 Monza 2+2 hatchback is equipped with the $521 Spyder option package, which added flashy spoilers and stripes.*

1976-1983 Chevette

Right: *Woody side trim, a roof rack, and deluxe wheel covers were among the dress-up items available for the '76 Chevette.* **Middle:** *A four-door hatchback body style was added to the Chevette lineup for '78. The 1982 four-door hatchback (shown here) cost $5238 in low-priced "Scooter" trim.*

Look. A lot more Chevette for a lot less money.

SEE WHAT'S NEW TODAY IN A CHEVROLET.

Right: *This '83 Chevette two-door has the S exterior package that exchanged chrome moldings for black-finish trim. Chevette sales peaked at 451,161 in '80, but were down to 169,565 in '83. Production ended in '87.*

After the oil embargo, American automakers scrambled to add small economy cars to their lines. Chevrolet turned to Opel, General Motors' German subsidiary, and developed an Americanized version of the Opel Kadett called Chevette. It arrived for '76 as a two-door hatchback with a petite 94.3-inch wheelbase, sub-2000-lb curb weight, and a 1.4-liter, 52-hp four-cylinder engine. Introduced in 1980, Citation was the first front-wheel-drive Chevrolet. Citation followed contemporary European small cars in having a compact powertrain situated "east-west" instead of the traditional "north-south." The result was a smaller exterior package with similar interior space versus the superseded Nova. Sales were strong initially, with 811,540 built the debut year. However, sales fell rapidly after safety recalls hurt Citation's reputation.

Above: *Among the formerly optional equipment made standard for '78 was the larger 1.6-liter/97.6-cid engine rated at 63 hp.*

1980-1985 Citation

Right: *A cutaway drawing shows the transverse-engine/front-drive layout of the '80 Citation two-door hatchback.* **Below, left:** *The four-door hatchback Citation II of 1984 was little changed from previous Citations.*

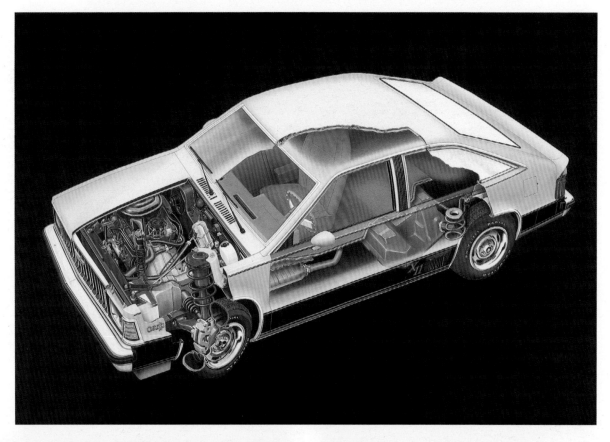

Below: *This '85 Citation II two-door hatchback is equipped with the X-11 package, which included a 135-hp, 173-cid V-6, firmer steering and suspension, and sporty exterior cosmetics.*

1982-1995 Cavalier

Right: *The '82 Cavalier lineup included notchback coupe (foreground), sedan, hatchback coupe, and wagon. A convertible was added in '83.*
Below, middle: *Cavalier got updated styling for '91. An RS sedan is shown.*

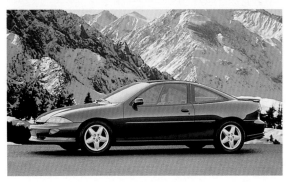

Right: *Cavalier got a long overdue redesign and fresh styling for '95. The wheelbase grew to 104.1 inches. Base Cavaliers had a 2.2-liter, 120-hp four, and a twin-cam four with 150 hp was available.*

Replacing Monza in '82 was the front-wheel-drive Cavalier. After the problems with Citation, Chevrolet made sure the Cavalier was right from the start. Cavalier had a trim 101.2-inch wheelbase and was initially powered by an 88-hp 1.8-liter four, which made for lackluster acceleration. In '83, a longer-stroke, 2.0-liter four helped some. Cavalier had decent room for four, neat styling, and competitive prices. The first-generation Cavalier soldiered on with regular updates until '95, when the line was completely redesigned. The Cavalier name was retired in mid-2005, when the long-serving '95-vintage basic design was phased out in favor of the all-new Chevrolet Cobalt. Base power for the Cobalt was a 2.2-liter four with a respectable 145 horsepower.

Top: *The sporty '89 Cavalier Z24 coupe was powered by a 2.8-liter, 130-hp V-6. Cavalier sales were 376,626 for the model year.* **Above:** *The RS was the sportier of two available Cavalier wagons for '91.*

2005-2009 Cobalt

Right: *The Cobalt was a huge improvement over the aged Cavalier. The sedan-only 2005 Cobalt LT model (shown) came well equipped with traction control, Pioneer sound system, leather upholstery, and heated front seats.*

Left: *The high-performance 2009 Cobalt SS coupe had a turbocharged 2.0-liter, 260-hp four and was capable of 0-60 mph in 5.7 seconds. A sport suspension, mandatory 5-speed manual transmission, and sporty styling add-ons enhanced the racy feel.*

CHAPTER FIVE

The Hot Ones

Detroit's postwar "horsepower race" had blossomed into a full-on hot-car craze by the early Sixties. Chevrolet was already near and dear to hot-rodders' hearts thanks to the classic 1955-57 Chevys, and the new-for-1961 Impala Super Sport package and 409 engine cemented the bond. Chevy was also quick to field effective responses to the two most-influential and successful youth-market cars of the day; the Chevelle SS 396 answered Pontiac's GTO, and the Camaro countered Ford's Mustang. Detroit performance went into hibernation as the Seventies dawned, but reemerged in the late 1980s and early 1990s thanks to advancing engine technology and better emissions controls. Chevrolet delighted performance enthusiasts and capitalized on its rich performance heritage with the reborn 1994-96 Impala SS and the retro-styled 2010 Camaro lineup.

Classic muscle car advertising was every bit as swaggering and boastful as the cars themselves. In the case of the 1970 Chevelle SS 396, the tough talk was justified.

Other cars wish the Chevelle SS 396 would hold still long enough for them to catch up.

Other cars wish the 1970 SS 396 hadn't added those 25 more horses to boost its standard V8 to 350 hp.

Other cars wish the SS 396 didn't offer you that new air-gulping Cowl Induction Hood.

Other cars wish the SS 396 didn't offer a 4-speed or a 3-range Turbo Hydra-matic transmission.

And other cars wish the stock SS 396 didn't give you power disc brakes, beefed-up suspension, F70 x 14 white-lettered wide ovals and 7"-wide sport wheels.

Aren't you glad other cars don't have anything to say about it?

On the move. CHEVROLET

Chevelle SS 396. Other cars wish we'd keep it this way.

1961-1964 Bel Air & Impala

Left and above: *This Impala convertible is equipped with two of 1961's most desirable options: the Super Sport package and 409 V-8.*

Below: *Lighter in weight and $100 cheaper than an Impala, the Bel Air sport coupe was a popular choice among 409 buyers in 1962. The base single-carb 409 had 380 hp; the dual-carb version put out 409 ponies.*

Chevrolet delivered a one-two punch with the mid-1961 introduction of the Impala Super Sport package and the soon-to-be-famous 409 V-8. The "SS" was an appearance package that included spinner wheel covers, a tachometer, heavy-duty shocks, upgraded brakes, special badging, and other extras. The 409 was basically a larger, stronger 348 intended to make Chevy a power in stock-car and drag racing (even though the division didn't officially compete in '61). The 409 was a formidable force in Super Stock drag racing competition and reigned as Chevy's top big-car powerplant until mid-1965, when it was replaced by the new big-block 396.

Right: *In 1963, Chevy built a limited number of "Z-11" Impalas with 427-cube engines and lightweight body panels for drag racing.* **Below:** *By '64, the hottest 409 was rated at a walloping 425 horsepower.*

if YOU LIKE PLAYING WITH BLOCKS, TRY THIS. With Chevrolet's Turbo-Fire 409 V8* block you can build to great heights. Say, 340 hp. 400 hp. Or, with the ingredients shown here, 425 hp. All three use the same block. Looks like the Rock of Gibraltar with 409 cubic inches of tunneling punched in it.

For the 425-hp 409 we add all those lovingly machined, cast and forged items above. Twin 4-barrel carburetors. Impact-extruded pistons. Forged steel connecting rods and five-main-bearing crankshaft. Cast alloy iron camshaft. And two heads fitted with lightweight valves. Mechanical valve lifters. Along with things we didn't show—header-type exhaust manifolds, dual exhausts, special clutch and heavy-duty radiator and suspension, among others. For the tamer 340- and 400-hp 409's, we use tamer bits and pieces here and there.

You can tuck a 425-hp Turbo-Fire 409 V8 into any '64 Chevrolet Biscayne, Bel Air, Impala or Impala Super Sport. And choose low gear ratios of 2.56:1 or 2.20:1 with the 4-speed all-synchro shift*. With the 2.20:1 gear ratio you can get 4.11:1 or 4.56:1 Positraction High Performance axle ratios*. Isn't playing with blocks fun?... Chevrolet Division of General Motors, Detroit, Michigan.

CHEVROLET

*Optional at extra cost.

Top, middle, and left: *As before, the Impala SS was the flashiest way to get 409 power. Output rose to 185,325 sport coupes (shown) and ragtops for 1964. Tri-bar spinner hubcaps were an Impala SS exclusive.*

1967-1968 Impala SS

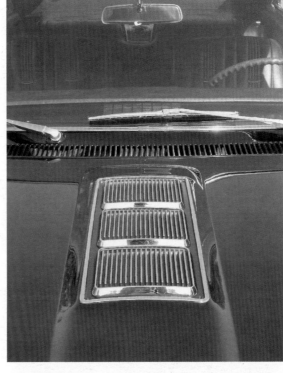

Left: *Chrome faux intake ports dressed up the hood of the '67 SS 427.* **Below:** *The Impala SS still had the headline position in this 1968 ad for Chevy's hot-car lineup, but it was being eclipsed by the smaller, lighter, and more affordable Chevelle, Camaro, and Nova SSs.*

Above, right, and bottom: *Chevy took its big-car performance a step further for 1967 with the Impala SS 427. Included were stiffer springs and shocks, a front stabilizer bar, redline tires, and a 385-hp 427.*

1994-1996 Impala SS

Right and far right: *Though down 40 hp from Corvette tune, the LT1 Impala SS V-8 could vault the 2-ton sedan from 0 to 60 mph in just 6.5 seconds on the way to a 15-second quarter-mile, according to* Car and Driver.

Left: *The Impala SS changed little over its three-year model run. Aggressive looks came courtesy of blacked-out trim, a lower ride height, and beefy tires on handsome five-spoke wheels.*

Chevy kept the full-size muscle fires burning in the late Sixties with its Impala Super Sport models—especially the brawny SS 427. However, sales for these big bruisers plummeted as the more-popular intermediate muscle cars took over, and SS would be dropped from the line after 1969. Enthusiasts didn't forget, however. In 1994, Chevy reintroduced the Impala SS name on a hot-rodded version of the Caprice Classic sedan, and the model gained an instant cult following.

Left: *The Impala SS got a floorshift automatic, analog speedometer, and standard tachometer for 1996, its final season.*

1967-1969 Camaro

Right, top: *Hidden headlamps identified Camaros equipped with the Rally Sport appearance package.* **Right, middle:** *Camaros were popular with hot rodders from the start, and even some Chevy dealers got into the act. Yenko Chevrolet in Pennsylvania produced a limited number of 427-powered Camaros like this one.* **Far right:** *Bowing in early '67, the Camaro Z-28 package was created for the Sports Car Club of America's Trans-American race series. Included were broad dorsal stripes, performance suspension, and a high-revving 302 V-8.*

COMMAND DRIVE A CAMARO TODAY!

CHEVROLET
GM

Left: *Chevrolet's pony car wasn't much altered for its sophomore year, but it did get flow-through "Astro Ventilation" instead of vent windows. Optional four-wheel disc brakes arrived at midyear and were especially welcome on the high-performance Z-28.*

Left: *The brawny 427 wasn't a regular Camaro option, but could be had in dealer specials like this Yenko/SC Camaro.* **Below:** *Production of the Camaro Z-28 nearly tripled for the 1969 model year, to 20,302.*

Above: *Camaros got a beefier look for '69 via new bodywork. "Hockey-stick" stripes were a sporty appearance option.* **Far right:** *The Rally Sport option package now featured hidden headlamps with triple-glass windows for "flash-to-pass" signaling. The headlamp covers powered aside for nighttime driving.*

Chevrolet's new-for-'67 Camaro answered the wildly successful Ford Mustang ponycar, and was a solid hit itself. The Camaro's enormous options list was daunting, but it enabled shoppers to create a mild-mannered cruiser, a swingin' performance machine, or anything in between. SS Camaros with a 295-hp 350 V-8 were available from the start, and a 375-hp 396 was added as an option later in the year. Meanwhile, the Z-28 Camaro brought road-race-ready hardware. Substantial restyling for 1969 brought more-muscular looks and even more performance and appearance choices. Any first-generation Camaro is highly sought after today.

1970-1992 Camaro

Separates the men from the toys.

Remember when you were a kid and you put a lot of trick stuff on your bike to make it look like something it wasn't?

A lot of so-called "sporty cars" still operate that way.

But not this one.

The new Camaro Z28 is as good looking underneath as it is on top.

With a 360-horse Turbo-Fire 350 V8. And with a Hurst shifter that comes along for the ride when you order the 4-speed.

Then there's the suspension that lets you feel the road without feeling the bumps. And the quick ratio steering. And the special wheels with the F60 x 15 tires. And on, and on, and on.

But don't just take our word for it. Pick one up at your Chevy dealer's Sports Department and take it for a road test.

You'll see we're not kidding around.

Putting you first, keeps us first.

CHEVROLET

Right: *Choosing the Z28 package added $573 to the cost of a '70 Camaro.* **Below:** *Rally Sport-equipped Camaros, like this '71 Z28, featured a distinctive split-bumper nose with round parking lights.*

Left: *The '70 Z28 packed a gutsy new 360-hp LT1 350 V-8.* **Below:** *New emissions regulations meant the '74 Z28s weren't as fast as their predecessors, but they still boasted striking looks and excellent handling.*

Camaro was totally redesigned for 1970, and despite a delayed introduction, the new car was another instant hit. Clever styling and engineering updates helped Chevrolet keep the basic second-generation Camaro design fresh for its lengthy 11-year lifespan. All-new third-generation Camaros debuted for 1982 with crisp new bodywork on a slimmer and trimmer platform. Once again, Chevy relied on regular upgrades to the core design to extend the third-gen Camaro's "shelf life" to just over a decade.

Left: *Z28 Camaros received another round of striping and trim revisions for 1980, including a new body-color horizontal bar grille, functional front-fender vents, and rear fender flares.* **Middle:** *Here, the 1982 Z28 fronts its '81 predecessor. The new Z's top engine choice was a fuel-injected 5.0-liter V-8 with 165 horsepower.*

Bottom: *Camaro turned 25 in 1992, and Chevrolet commemorated the occasion with a Heritage Appearance package that included bold hood and decklid stripes and a decklid badge.*

Above: *The 1977 Camaro Z28 packed plenty of high-performance hardware.* **Right:** *The top-line Camaro IROC-Z (a 1986 model is shown here) got its name from the International Race of Champions series.*

1993-2010 Camaro

Right: *The 1993 Camaro was all-new and much improved, but retained many of the aggressive styling cues of its predecessor.*
Far right: *Interiors were improved as well, with better ergonomics and standard dual front airbags.*

Left: *A tradition continued: The 1996 Camaro Brickyard 400 poses at the famed Indianapolis Motor Speedway with the '67, '69, '82, and '93 Indy 500 pace Camaros.*

Above: *The end of an era: the 2002 farewell-edition 35th Anniversary Camaros came as SS ragtops or T-top coupes in red only, with special wheels and stripes.*

A fresh, fully-redesigned Camaro debuted for 1993, dazzling the public and press alike. The new car got off to a great start, but sales began to sputter as the years wore on. By the dawn of the 21st century, most of Chevrolet's resources were focused on more-popular (and more-profitable) SUV models. The Camaro was deemed expendable and was dropped after the 2002 model year. Then, rival Ford introduced an all-new, retro-styled Mustang as a 2005 model and proceeded to light up the sales charts. Chevy couldn't let this challenge go unanswered, and rolled out a showstopping Camaro Concept at the 2006 Detroit Auto Show. This new heritage-themed Camaro was greenlighted for production soon after, and after an eight-year hiatus, new Camaros arrived again as 2010 models.

Top left: *This cutaway illustration by David Kimble displays the sophisticated innards of the 2010 Camaro SS.* **Top:** *Camaro SSs packed a muscular 6.2-liter V-8 that boasted 422 hp with the 6-speed manual transmission, or 400 with the 6-speed automatic. Sinister "halo ring" high-intensity headlamps were included with the Rally Sport appearance package.* **Middle and bottom:** *Camaro LTs (seen here in Victory Red and Rally Yellow) were powered by a 300-hp 3.6-liter V-6.*

1966-1967 Chevelle SS/Nova SS

Right: *This eye-catching brochure was issued to Chevy dealers to help them sell the gutsy 396 V-8 models.*
Far right: *The training must have worked, as sales were healthy for '66; some 72,300 Chevelle SS 396 hardtops (shown) and convertibles were built.*

Far left and bottom left: *A blackout grille and unique hood with nonfunctional vents were SS 396 exclusives.* **Left:** *The air-cleaner sticker and bare-aluminum intake manifold indicate that this SS 396 is equipped with the top engine option: the 375-hp L78 396. Only about 3100 '66 Chevelles were so equipped.*

Right: *After a 1966 restyle that gave it a tougher look, the Chevy II Nova saw only minor trim changes for '67.*
Far right and below: *SS 396 Chevelles priced from a reasonable $2825 for 1967. The optional five-spoke wheel covers shown here mimicked the look of popular after-market "mag" wheels.*

General Motors' Pontiac division kick-started the muscle-car craze with the 1964 Pontiac GTO, but Chevy wasn't far behind. After a limited run of 396-powered "Z-16" Chevelles for 1965, big-block muscle became an official part of the Chevelle lineup with the 1966 SS 396 models. A 325-hp 396 was standard, but hotter 360- and 375-hp versions were available. Though still set on the original Chevelle chassis, the '66 featured sleek new styling with an eager, forward-leaning front profile and a "flying buttress" two-door hardtop roof with a recessed rear window. A smart facelift for 1967 brought a new grille, wraparound taillights, and other styling updates. Meanwhile, the compact Chevy II/Nova was growing into its own as a budget hot car; 1966 brought a handsome restyle and the availability of the 350-hp L79 327 V-8. With their favorable power-to-weight ratio, these pint-size powerhouses could surprise many big-block-powered rivals.

1968-1969 Chevelle SS/Nova SS

Right and far right: *Chevelle's slick new look for '68 naturally lent itself to the SS 396's sporty styling touches. In coupe form, SS 396s started at $2899. The 375-hp 396 added another $237.*

Right and above: *Nova SSs could be distinguished by their blackout grille/taillight-panel treatments and faux hood vents. Small front marker-light badges are the tip-off that this '69 model is 396-powered.*

Right: *Chevrolet was eager to show that the formerly mild-mannered Nova wasn't so mild anymore.* **Top and middle:** *Chevrolet dealer Don Yenko swapped Chevy's mighty 427 into the 1969 Nova to create one of the hairiest muscle cars ever. Just 37 were produced.* **Bottom:** *As expected, Chevelle's year-old styling was just mildly tweaked for 1969. SS 396 production hit a new one-year high of 86,307 units.*

The Sleeper Awakes

'69 Chevy Nova SS. Up and at 'em!
Louvers on the front fenders, a bulging hood and a throbbing exhaust note let people know this one's no imitation.
Backing up a standard 300-hp V8 is a muscular foundation: special suspension, an extra-tough clutch, red stripe wide ovals on 7" wide wheels, a special 3-speed and power disc brakes.
The '69 Chevy Nova SS, the car that woke up swinging.

Putting you first, keeps us first. CHEVROLET

Both the Chevelle and Chevy II/Nova were redesigned for 1968 along a similar styling theme, with swept-back C-pillars and a sloping rear deck. Novas were now available with big-block power as well; the 396 was added to the options list partway through the 1968 season. For both the Chevelle and Nova SSs, the 375-hp L78 396 was "officially" the top engine available. For speed-crazy buyers who craved even more, Chevrolet "unofficially" produced a limited number of 1969 Chevelles with factory-installed 427s. Plus, a handful of high-performance Chevy dealers around the country were swapping 427s into Chevelles and Novas to create their own supercars.

1970-1972 Chevelle SS

Right and below: *The 1970 Chevelle SS 454 was a definite high-water mark in the muscle-car era. The solid-lifter LS6 454 was the hottest engine, rated at a whopping 450 hp. An optional cowl induction hood drew air from the base of the windshield via a vacuum-controlled flap.*
Far right: *Squarer lines for 1970 gave SS Chevelles the stance of a street tough, and Chevrolet's evocative advertising photography only heightened the effect.*

1970 Chevelle SS 396.
It's getting tougher and tougher to resist.
The standard V8 has been kicked up to 350 hp.
A new air-gulping Cowl Induction Hood awaits your order.
You can also order your choice of a floor-mounted 4-speed or the 3-range Turbo Hydra-matic.
Under that lean and hungry look is a lean and agile suspension. F70 x 14 white-lettered wide oval treads. 7"-wide mag-type wheels. And power disc brakes.
Your mission is to infiltrate your Chevy dealer's and escape with this car.
It will go willingly.
Putting you first, keeps us first.

CHEVROLET
On the move.

In ten seconds, your resistance will self-destruct.

The age of muscle peaked in 1970, and Chevelle was there to herald its ascent. SS 396s were still available, but the new king of the hill was the SS 454. In top-dog LS6 form, the 454 V-8 put out a barbaric 450 horsepower—the highest factory hp rating of the day. Soon, spiraling insurance costs, tightening emissions regulations, and a changing social climate would bring the muscle-car era to a close. Chevy saw the handwriting on the wall, and began detuning its high-performance engines for 1971. Most enthusiasts regard 1972 as the last year for "true" Detroit muscle cars in the original 1960s mold.

Left and below: *This Cream Yellow coupe is one of 24,946 SS Chevelles built for 1972. Of those, a mere 300 left the factory with the 454 big-block, which was now rated at just 270 hp.*

Above: *Chevrolet offered a "Heavy Chevy" appearance package for the 1971 Chevelle as a low-budget option for the costlier SS models.*
Right: *SS 454 Chevelles survived into 1971, but in tamer form. Convertibles like this one retailed for around $4700.*

109

CHAPTER SIX

Fiberglass Flyers

Corvette, Chevrolet's answer to the postwar sports car boom, made its first appearance at the 1953 General Motors Motorama exhibition. After an enthusiastic reception, the two-seat, fiberglass-bodied roadster was rushed to production. Early 'Vettes were lackluster performers, but by the late Fifties, chief engineer Zora Arkus-Duntov's hard work—along with Chevy's small-block V-8—had transformed Corvette into a true American sports car. Corvette epitomized the muscular excesses of the Sixties and even thrived during the emissions-control challenges of the Seventies. The Eighties infused the 'Vette with increasingly sophisticated technology. The Nineties brought a major rework of the small-block engine and steadily climbing horsepower. As the new millennium progressed, Corvette offered unprecedented levels of refinement and performance.

Corvette styling was always daring and flamboyant. The new styling for '68, based on the Mako Shark II show car, was quite controversial at the time. However, sales still set a new record of 28,566.

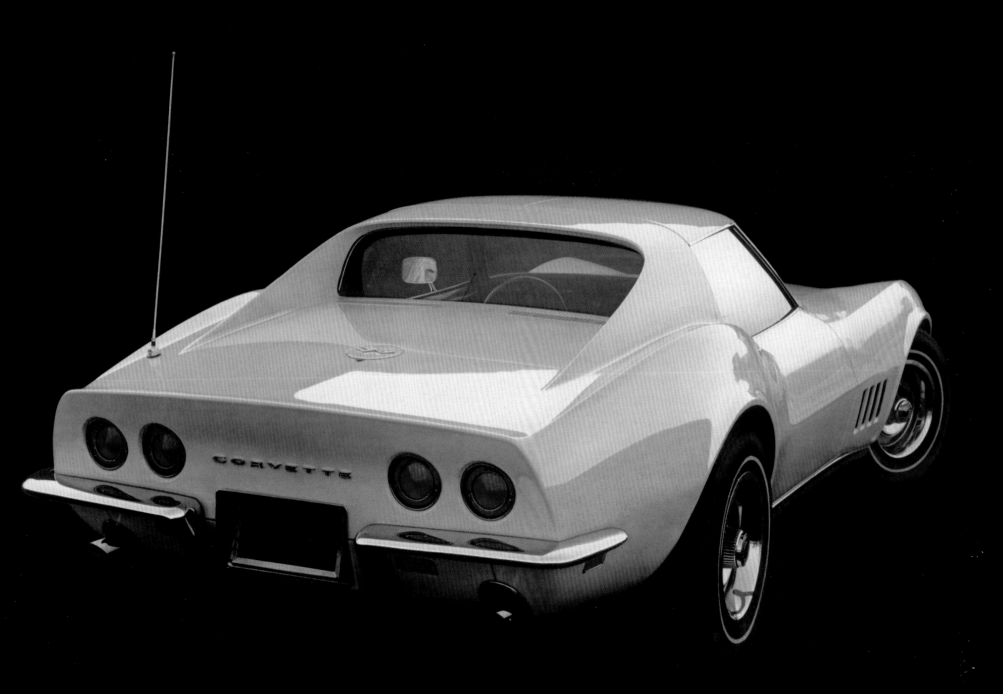

1953-1957

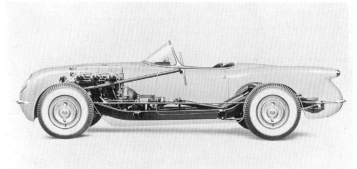

Above: *First-year 'Vette production was limited to 300, and all of those were white with red interiors.* **Right:** *The Corvette version of the '55 Chevy V-8 used a special camshaft to unleash another 33 horsepower, for a total of 195.*

The first Corvettes were more "show" than "go." Chevrolet's sports car had to make do with Chevy's venerable inline six and 2-speed "Powerglide" automatic. Chevy's small-block V-8 arrived in '55 with 195 horsepower from 265 cubic inches. That, along with a new three-speed manual transmission, gave Corvette credible performance. Dazzling new styling arrived for '56, while newly hired engineer Zora Arkus-Duntov made the handling more capable. For '57, the V-8 grew to 283 cid and horsepower ratings went as high as 283, courtesy of the newly optional "Ramjet" fuel injection.

Top: *The '53 Corvette's engine was mounted behind the front axle for better balance.* **Above:** *A V-8-powered '55 'Vette could sprint from 0 to 60 mph in 8.5 seconds.*

Right: *The '56 Corvette was available with a newly optional hardtop.*
Far right: *Zora Arkus-Duntov kicked up some sand at Daytona with this test Corvette prior to '56 runs on the famed beach. Arkus-Duntov managed a two-way run of 150.583 mph during Daytona Speed Weeks.*

"FANTASTICO! EVEN IN TURIN NO ONE HAS FUEL INJECTION!"

Sì, è vero. But the really fantastic item about the new Corvette is not the fuel injection engine, the new four-speed gearbox,* the slingshot acceleration or the pasted-to-the-road stability. It is the fact that the Corvette, above all other high-performance sports cars in the world, is a true dual-natured vehicle. It is a genuine luxury car and a genuine sports car, both wrapped in one sleek skin.

This is something like a panther with a St. Bernard's disposition. Quite a trick, but what a pet! But, in case you may have polite doubts about the Corvette's uniqueness, we have an easy rebuttal: Drive one!

In point of fact, we have no further enticement. If you can spend half an hour in the deep-cushioned comfort of a Corvette's cockpit, if you can sample the crispness of its controls, the veracity of its 16 to 1 steering, the incredible crescendo of its performance—and remain unshaken—you are mighty close to being unique. Frankly, very few drivers escape the feeling that this is one of the authentic great moments of motoring—and those few are not warm to the touch! . . . Chevrolet Division of General Motors, Detroit 2, Michigan.

SPECIFICATIONS: Blue-absolute V8 engine with single four-barrel carburetor, 220 h.p. (four other engines* range to 283 h.p. with fuel injection). Close-ratio three-speed manual transmission standard, with special Powerglide automatic drive* available on all but maximum-performance engines. Choice of removable hard top or power-operated fabric top.* Power-Lift windows.* Instruments include tach-o-meter, oil pressure gauge and ammeter. *Optional at extra cost.

CORVETTE *by Chevrolet*

Right: *Many 1957 Corvette ads poked fun at the 'Vette's European rivals. Fuel-injection was expensive at around $500, so orders were few.*

Left and middle: *Discreet lettering in the concave bodyside "coves" signals this car is one of 1040 fuel-injection equipped '57 Corvettes. Relatively few '57s had monotone paint.*

1958-1962

The 1958 Corvette had new styling, but the chassis was little changed. Wheelbase remained 102 inches, but overall length grew 10 inches. Weight increased, but so did engine power. Production for '58 rose to 9168, and Corvette had its first profitable year. In 1960, the most powerful fuel-injected V-8 was putting out 290 hp and sales topped 10,000 for the first time. By '61, even the mildest engine teamed with a Powerglide automatic was good for 0-60 mph in 7.7 seconds. Performance with 315-hp "fuelie" and four-speed manual was 0-60 in 5.5 seconds and a top speed of 130-mph plus. For '62, engine size was increased to 327 cid and horsepower ranged from 250 to 360. Styling had been getting progressively cleaner with less chrome, and the '62 'Vette was the most cohesive design of its generation.

Above left: *Chrome decklid "suspenders" were a '58-only design detail.* **Above right:** *The buying public must have liked Corvette's new styling for '58. Corvette was one of the few cars to see increased sales during that recession year.* **Left:** *The 1960 Corvette looked virtually identical to the '59, and the base price actually dropped a few dollars, to $3872.*

Right: *Sunvisors were newly standard on '61 Corvettes.* **Far right top:** *An all-new flowing ducktail rear end was the '61 Corvette's biggest change. Increased luggage space was a bonus of the slick new look.*

Right: *Corvette won its first B-Production championship in Sports Car Club of America racing in 1962. Here, driver Don Yenko's number 10 and Dr. Dick Thompson's number 11 get ready for a three-hour contest at Daytona.* **Far right middle and far right bottom:** *The 1962 Corvette's price rose to $4038, and production soared to 14,531.*

1963-1964

Above: *The shark-like '63 Corvettes were christened "Sting Ray." They were the first American cars with hidden headlights since the 1942 DeSoto.*

ONLY A MAN WITH A HEART OF STONE COULD WITHSTAND TEMPTATION LIKE THIS. You can wear a blindfold, have your wife tie you to the old family sedan, lock up the checkbook, anything of the kind; but Mister, if you ever hankered to buy a sports car, you're about to become the owner of a new Corvette Sting Ray. Sensible talk about the family budget, the good years left in your present car, any kind of rational thought, forget it! Here's why: The new Corvette Sting Ray, available in sport coupe or traditional convertible model, takes all the excellent characteristics of earlier Corvettes and multiplies them by two. The previous Corvette was the world's most exciting sports car for the last five years, and this new one shows every indication of keeping the title for the *next* five. It has fully independent rear suspension, bigger self-adjusting brakes, retractable headlights, a V8 engine that's prettier than most girls, and new extra-cost options like a four-speed all-synchro transmission, knock-off aluminum wheels, monstrous finned aluminum brake drums with metallic linings, and Fuel Injection for 360 horsepower. Combine all this with a seating position and a seat-of-the-pants driving sensation like nothing you ever felt, and you've got a car that absolutely will not be denied. And if you're interested enough to have read all this, you might as well stop by the bank on your way to the Chevrolet dealer's. It's fate, man. . . . Chevrolet Division of General Motors, Detroit 2, Mich.

New CORVETTE STING RAY by Chevrolet

Above left: *The '63 'Vette was well received by the public; sales totaled 21,513.* **Above right:** *Sting Rays featured a more comfortable cockpit dominated by a new "twin cowl" dashboard.* **Left:** *GM styling honcho Bill Mitchell insisted on a controversial split rear window for the '63 coupes.*

Right: *For '64, the coupe's split rear window was replaced by a one piece rear window for improved visibility. Sting Rays lacked a traditional trunklid; the only access to the storage area was through the passenger compartment.* **Far right:** *Corvette convertibles outsold coupes 13,925 to 8304 in '64.*

The new Sting Ray of 1963 was the first complete revision of Corvette since its introduction 10 years earlier. Powertrains and front suspension were carried over, but everything else was new. General Motors styling chief Bill Mitchell made Sting Ray a pet project, and the results were stunning. The convertible was joined by the first-ever Corvette coupe. Chief engineer Zora Arkus-Duntov oversaw development of a new chassis and insisted on independent rear suspension instead of a solid rear axle. Arkus-Duntov did his work well, and that basic chassis, with revisions, would serve Corvette ably through 1982. The 327-cid small-block V-8s were carried over for the Sting Ray and provided more than enough power in the more aerodynamic new Corvette. The Sting Ray proved the fastest, most-roadable 'Vette yet.

Just a minute! That's a '64 Corvette Sting Ray those two deserted to go perch on an everyday old rock and gaze at the piney woods! Ah well, love is seldom rational. Saner souls would harken to Corvette's windswept '64 styling, clean as the Sport Coupe's new one-piece rear window. They'd take to that dressed-up interior—new simulated walnut-rim steering wheel, new instrument faces, redesigned center console, an interior ventilator in Sport Coupe models to boost air circulation. People with both feet on the ground would hoist them aboard to sample Corvette's quieter, smoother ride; the muffled thunder of a V8 in one of four versions up to 375 hp*; or the joys of a new 4 speed manual transmission*, improved standard 3-speed or Powerglide automatic*. Clear thinkers know there are two Corvettes, the Sport Coupe above and the Convertible, plus a long list of comfort, convenience and performance options. No use telling all this to that Sweet Young Thing and her swain. Anyway, you're the one that we—and your Chevrolet dealer—are really interested in. . . . Chevrolet Division of General Motors, Detroit, Michigan.   *OPTIONAL AT EXTRA COST

'64 CORVETTE STING RAY BY CHEVROLET

Left: *For '64, Arkus-Duntov was able to smooth out the ride with redesigned shock absorbers and variable-rate springs.* **Above:** *New wheel covers and less chrome marked '64 Sting Rays.*

1965-1967

Below and bottom left: *Chevy's new 427 big-block V-8 replaced the 396 as 1966's top power option, offering 390 or 425 hp. Doors wrapped into the roof to ease entry on Corvette coupes.*

Above: *The 396-cid big-block V-8 made its debut in '65. Optional alloy wheels were held in place by knock-off center hubs.* **Left:** *The convertible was again the most popular '65 'Vette, with 15,378 sold versus only 8186 coupes.*

Right: *Slotted Rally wheels made their first appearance in '67, replacing traditional hubcaps. All 427-equipped cars received a scooped hood with a "stinger" stripe. Many enthusiasts regard the '67 Sting Ray as one of the best 'Vettes of all time.* **Far right top and middle:** *The mighty 427 received a new triple two-barrel carb setup that was good for up to 435 hp.* **Far right bottom:** *This '67 coupe has the optional side exhaust pipes that could be ordered on 427-equipped Corvettes.*

After the major redesign for '63, Corvette would see only minor, but useful, refinements through '67. For '65, 327-cid small-block V-8s were joined by 396-cid big-block V-8s. In '66, the 396 grew to 427 cid and was rated at 390- or 425-horsepower, but many believe it was understated for better insurance rates and that 420 and 450 are closer to the truth. *Sports Car Graphic* managed to launch a 425-hp test car from 0 to 60 in an astonishing 4.8 seconds. Fuel-injected engines were dropped after 1965 because of limited demand. Four-wheel disc brakes became standard in '65 and were needed to match the steadily escalating performance. Corvettes were getting better every year, and the public appreciated it—sales reached a record 27,720 in 1966.

1968-1973

Above: *A special domed hood provided clearance for the hefty 427 big-block V-8 on '68 Corvettes.* **Above right:** *GM design chief Bill Mitchell poses with his 1965 Mako Shark II concept (left) and a red '68 convertible with optional hardtop.*

Left: *In 1969, Corvette sales increased to a record 38,762.* **Below:** *The '69s' steering-wheel diameter was trimmed an inch, and inner door panels were made thinner to address complaints about interior room.*

'70 Corvette.   What else.

Here it is. It's not really a whole lot different looking. But in 17 years, we've never changed it just to change it.

And there's one thing that hasn't changed at all.

The Corvette idea.

It's still a car that's built for the person who drives for the sheer excitement of it. For the driver who enjoys the true feel of the road.

Yet, it's still a car you can drive at 10 mph in a traffic jam.

It's still a car you can swing out to the beach in. Or pull up in front of a theater with your girl dressed to the teeth.

No, it isn't a hard-core sports car. There are too many nice things about it. It was made to perform. And it does just that.

No, it's not the smoothest riding car you'll find. But then again, it won't rattle your bones.

What it is is a new Corvette. It's refined for '70. The 4-Speed is standard. So is tinted glass. There are even a couple of new engines. All the way up to the 460-hp Turbo-Jet 454.

But if we know you, you'll find out all that for yourself.

We just want you to know it's here.

And it's one of those few cars that aren't something else.

Putting you first, keeps us first.

See it, Feb. 26th. At your Chevrolet Sports Dept.

CHEVROLET

GM

Left: *For 1972, the horsepower of the base 350-cid V-8 dropped from 270 to 200. This reflected tighter emissions standards and an industry switch from SAE gross to more-realistic net ratings.* **Left middle:** *For 1973, the Stingray coupe retained its trademark T-tops, but the rear window was no longer removable.*

Above: *A bigger 454-cid V-8 with 390 hp replaced the 427 V-8 for 1970. "Cheese grater" grille inserts were also new.* **Right:** *In 1973, a reshaped nose with a stronger bumper covered in body-color plastic was added to meet the government's new 5-mph bumper rule.*

The Corvette that arrived for 1968 looked all new, but in reality it was a new body and interior mounted on the chassis first introduced in 1963. The new styling, which was quite controversial at the time, lifted design cues from 1965's Mako Shark II show car. The Sting Ray moniker was dropped for a year, but it returned as one word—"Stingray"—in 1969. Coupes now sported a pair of lift-out panels called "T-tops" and removable rear window glass. The new interior featured a distinctive dash but provided less space. The previous year's engine choices carried over for '68, but the 327 increased capacity to 350 cid in '69 and the 427 grew to 454 cid in '70.

1974-1982

Right: In spite of the oil embargo, Corvette production rose to 37,502 units in '74. However, the once-mighty 454 was down to just 270 hp and would be dropped after this year. **Far right:** A new-for-'77 decklid luggage carrier could store the detached roof panels. Since '74, Corvette's 5-mph rear bumper was sheathed in body-colored plastic.

The Silver Anniversary Corvette.

25 years of men, machines, and memories.

It stands alone today as it has since the summer of 1953, a truly unique and finely machined two-seater, America's only true production sports car.

The legend lives on and improves, as legends do, with the passage of time.

The Silver Anniversary Corvette: Twenty-five years in the making, and we've enjoyed every minute of it.

And now, if you will, please join us in a round of applause for the Corvette founding fathers, that spirited corps of doers and dreamers who created the legend, brought it to life, and kept it there.

Also for the countless men and women who've had a hand in building and refining Corvettes over the years. For everyone who has ever owned a Corvette, driven one, loved one. Or dreamed about owning one someday.

Which, we'd imagine, includes just about everybody.

SEE WHAT'S NEW TODAY IN A CHEVROLET.

Chevrolet

Far left: Posing with the '78 Corvette Indianapolis 500 Pace Car are (clockwise from left) Corvette chief engineer David R. McClellan, Chevy engineers Paul J. King and Robert Stempel, and Chevy General Manager Robert Lund. **Left:** Corvette celebrated its 25th anniversary in 1978 with freshened styling and a new "fastback-style" wraparound rear window.

Right: *For '79, the base 350 V-8 got a less-restrictive air cleaner, which helped boost power by 10 hp, to 195. The optional L82 V-8 gained 5 hp to 225. Interior revisions included a standard AM/FM radio and seats similar to those used in the '78 Indy pace car replica.*

Left: *Chevy put Corvette on a diet for better performance and fuel economy. One hundred fifty pounds were shed in 1980, and this '81 coupe lost another 100 pounds. Also in '81, Corvette production moved to Bowling Green, Kentucky.*

Left and below: *The '82 Corvette had the first fuel-injection system since '65. A $22,538 Collector Edition marked the last production year for the '68 bodystyle.*

Chevrolet found itself in difficult times as it tried to meet increasingly stringent government standards and sell Corvettes in an era of soaring gas prices. In '75, base horsepower dropped to 165—the lowest since the 1953-55 six. Inflation was also a problem, with the price of a base 'Vette rising from $6002 in '74 to $18,290 in '82. Yet sales were strong, with a record 53,807 'Vettes sold in 1979. A mid-engined replacement for the Stingray was developed, but high production costs killed the project. Instead, the '68 design had to carry on through '82. Along the way, Corvette dropped the 454-cid V-8 after '74, discontinued the convertible in '75, and dropped the Stingray name after '76.

1984-1989

Right: *Chevy considered the 1984 Corvette a fourth design generation and informally designated it "C4." The former T-tops were replaced by a one-piece, lift-off roof panel.*

Left: *Tuned-port injection was adopted for the 1985 edition of the Corvette 350-cid V-8.* **Below:** *Corvette's reborn roadster cost $32,032 and found 7315 buyers in 1986.*

Above: *A large "clamshell" hood gave excellent engine access. The lift-up glass hatch provided access to the trunk.* **Right:** *Famed aviator Chuck Yeager drove a stock 'Vette pace car on the opening lap of the '86 Indy 500.*

Above: *For 1988, Corvette's horsepower rose to 245. The engine remained at 350 cubic inches, but by now it was more frequently described by its metric displacement of 5.7 liters.*

For the first time since 1963, Corvette was completely new. Development delays with the redesigned 'Vette forced Chevrolet to skip the 1983 model year, and it debuted as an '84. The new car proved worth the wait. The 350-cid V-8 with Cross-Fire Injection carried over, but almost everything else was new. The old perimeter-type frame was replaced by a new "integral perimeter-birdcage unitized structure." In effect, Corvette now employed unibody construction using a steel skeleton fitted with fiberglass panels. The base price jumped to $21,800, but production soared to 51,547. For '85, a switch from throttle-body to multiport fuel injection boosted horsepower to 230. In '86, a convertible returned to the Corvette lineup and paced the Indianapolis 500. That year, all Corvettes benefited from standard antilock brakes.

Above: *The '88 Corvette 35th Anniversary package was easily spotted by its black roof with white lower body and wheels.* **Left:** *Chevy revived a tradition for 1989 by offering a detachable hardtop for the Corvette convertible.*

1990-1996

Right: *ZR-1's LT5 was an all-aluminum V-8 with dual-overhead cams, 32 valves, and a tight 11.25:1 compression ratio.* **Far right:** *At $58,995, the 1990 ZR-1 was the most expensive GM car ever, but speculators bid that up to more than $100,000 for early examples.*

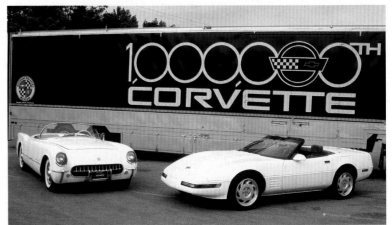

Left: *The ZR-1 (left) was broader in the back and sported different taillights in a convex instead of concave panel.* **Above:** *The landmark 1,000,000th Corvette left the Bowling Green production line on July 2, 1992.*

Below: *Corvette was once again named Indianapolis 500 pace car, this time for the 79th running of the race in 1995. Chevrolet ran off 527 replicas as a $2816 option package for the convertible.*

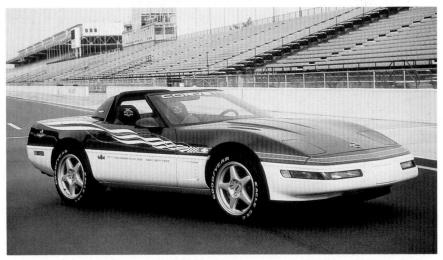

Above and top right: *The "King of the Hill" ZR-1 roared off into the sunset after 1995 and a final 448 examples. ZR-1 demand fell off rapidly after the first year.*

A "King of the Hill" Corvette was rumored for at least two years before Chevrolet released official details in 1989. Named ZR-1, this ultra-high-performance Corvette went on sale as a 1990 model. The ZR-1 was a $27,016 option package for Corvette coupes, boosting the list price to a staggering $58,995. The heart of the ZR-1 was an exotic new 5.7-liter LT5 V-8 that came mated to a six-speed manual transmission. Built for Chevrolet by Mercury Marine, the all-aluminum LT5 was rated at a thumping 375 horsepower. All 1990 Corvettes gained a standard driver-side airbag and a new dashboard. Corvette's standard 5.7-liter V-8 was thoroughly reworked for 1992—the re-engineered powerplant, dubbed LT1, put out 300 hp. To keep well ahead of the standard 'Vette, ZR-1 horsepower increased to 405 for '93. ZR-1 production ended in '95 after a total run of 6939 cars.

Left: *The Grand Sport package of '96 included a 330-hp LT4 V-8, special color scheme, and unique interior. The name and look recalled the racing Sting Rays developed by Zora Arkus-Duntov in 1963.*

1997-2004

This page: *Corvette was only available as a coupe for '97. A wide tail provoked some debate, but it helped the aerodynamic C5 achieve an admirable drag factor of only 0.29. A new iteration of the traditional "twin cowl" Corvette dash dominated the C5's roomier cockpit. Improvements included wider footwells and easy-to-read analog gauges.*

The all-new 1997 "C5" Corvette put a slinky new body on a more rigid uniframe. Wheelbase grew 8.3 inches to 104.5, the longest in 'Vette history, and length was up 1.2 inches, yet curb weight fell by about 80 pounds. A 5.7-liter pushrod V-8 remained the only powerplant, but it too was all new. A successful update of proven concepts, the 345-horsepower LS1 boasted aluminum cylinder heads and block. The C5 was the first Corvette with a rear-mounted transaxle. This arrangement helped the car achieve an ideal 50/50 front-to-rear weight balance. Prices started at $37,495, and production totaled 9752 in the shortened sales year. For '01, a new Z06 hardtop joined the line with a 385-hp V-8 and performance suspension.

Right: *The C5 'Vette gained a convertible for 1998, shown here with the Indy Pace Car Replica package.* **Far right:** *A new bodystyle for '99 was the hardtop, which featured a solid one-piece roof instead of the removable panel found on the coupe. The simpler construction offered greater rigidity and a 92-pound weight reduction.*

Left: *The 50th Anniversary Edition was an option for '03.* **Above:** *Z06 horsepower jumped to 405 in '02. This '04 has a Commemorative Edition paint scheme.*

2005-2010

Far left: *With the introduction of the new C6, Corvette production rose 10 percent, to 37,372 units, for 2005.* **Left top:** *New options for 2005 included XM satellite radio ($395) and a navigation system ($1800).* **Left middle:** *As always, the new-generation 'Vette was packed with plenty of high-tech hardware. Note the front brake-cooling air ducts behind the front fascia in this cutaway illustration.*

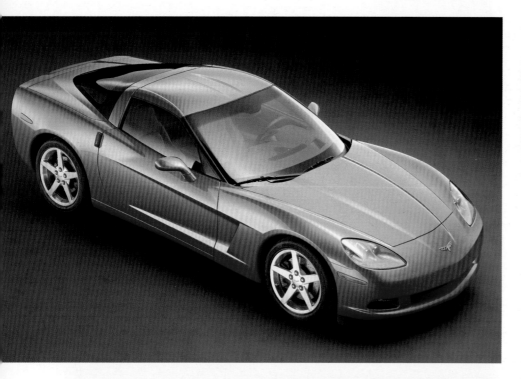

More an evolution of the C5 than an all-new car, the 2005 Corvette "C6" took giant steps forward in performance and refinement. The body was completely new, yet unmistakably a Corvette. Designers abandoned the hideaway headlamps that had been a Corvette staple since 1963, but some classic Sting Ray influence was visible in the peaked fender shapes. Under the hood was a 400-horsepower 6.0-liter LS2 engine—a bored-out version of the LS1 that debuted in the 1997 Corvette. The base price of the coupe was $43,710, while the convertible started at $52,245. Chevrolet revived the ultra-performance Z06 model on the C6 platform for 2006. The new Z06's engine displaced 7.0 liters and was rated at an astounding 505 horsepower. Z06 pricing started at $64,890.

Left: *The 2005 C6 was engineered to be a convertible from the start, so the droptops needed no additional underbody reinforcement. Corvette's power convertible top was a $1995 option.*

Right and far right:
The 2006 Z06 could be identified by its nose-mounted air intake and rear-brake cooling scoops, fixed roof, flared fenders, and monster 275/35ZR18 front and 325/30ZR19 rear tires. To save weight, Z06's uniframe was aluminum rather than the steel used in other 'Vettes.

Below left: *The 2010 Grand Sport had unique styling cues, along with sport suspension tuning and upgraded brakes.*
Below: *First shown at the 2009 Chicago Auto Show, the Stingray concept car hinted at the design features of future production Corvettes.*

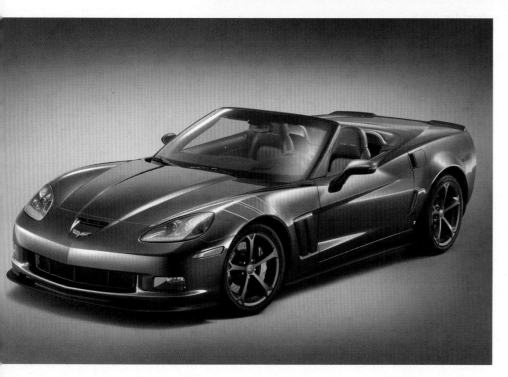

CHAPTER SEVEN

Call Me a Cop

Chevrolet has always been a basic, value-priced brand, so it's not at all surprising that Chevrolets were and are the vehicles of choice for many law-enforcement agencies. The typical police car leads a much harder life than the average civilian vehicle, so Chevrolet's reputation for reliability and durability is an important asset for police-fleet buyers. Plus, the clean styling of the typical Chevrolet simply looks natural "in uniform," with standard police equipment such as roof-mounted flashers, sirens, radios with thick exterior-mounted antennas, spotlights, and front-bumper push bars. From the bulletproof "stovebolt" sixes of yore to today's sturdy Impalas and Tahoes, Chevrolets have long served as trusted companions to America's men and women in uniform.

Heavy-duty steel wheels, speed-rated tires, over-sized sway bars, and a high-output alternator were just a few of the special components of the 9C1 police package for the 1996 Caprice Classic.

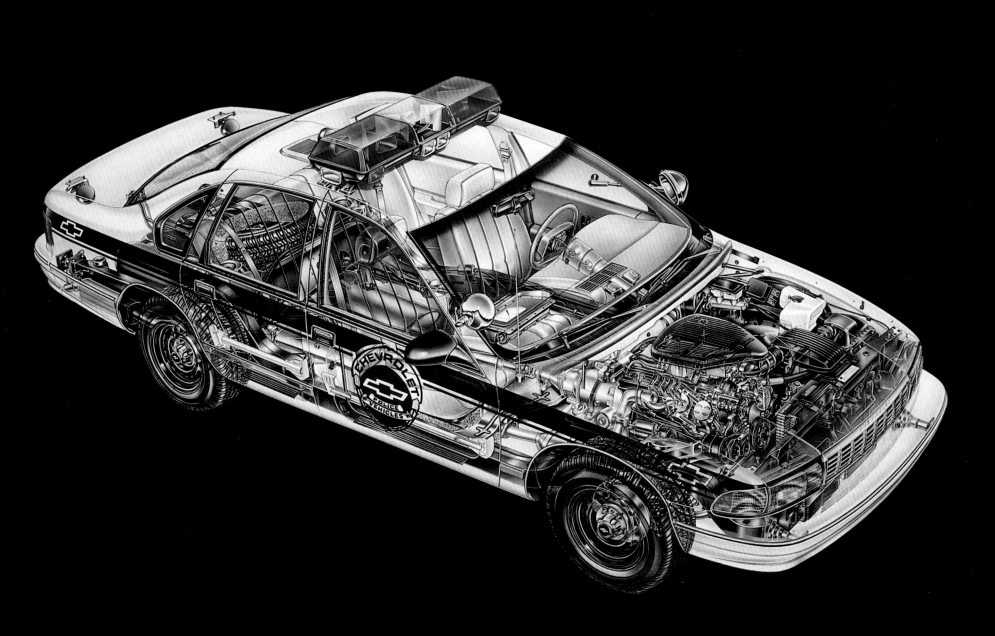

1947-1955

Though V-8 power kept Ford the low-priced performance leader from 1932 to 1955, law-enforcement agencies also used dependable Chevrolets—at least for tasks that didn't involve high-speed chases. The venerable Chevrolet "Stovebolt" six was reliable and easily repaired—traits very important to the smooth operation of a police fleet. By the mid-Fifties, Chevrolet and other manufacturers had developed dedicated "police-package" vehicles. These were usually base-model cars equipped at the factory with heavy-duty radiators, upgraded suspensions and electrical systems, and other components designed to withstand the rigors of police duty.

Top left and right: *The state of Idaho must have had money to burn in 1947, as it chose a $1313 Fleetline Aerosedan, Chevy's most-expensive two-door sedan, as a highway patrol car.* **Left:** *Michigan State Police cars, such as this '51 Styleline Special two-door sedan, used a unique stop sign mounted lengthwise on the hood.*

Right, below, and bottom: *This 1952 Styleline DeLuxe four-door sedan is an exact replica of a Macomb County Michigan Sheriff Patrol car, right down to the lights, period-correct radio, shotgun, and front-bumper guards.*

Left: *With its potent new Turbo-Fire V-8, Chevy was not only a much stronger rival to Ford for street performance in 1955 but a serious new challenger for police-car business. The one problem was keeping up with the much faster new V-8-powered Corvettes.*

1958-1966

POLICE
12743

Right and top right: *Chevrolets were the brand of choice for many state and municipal police agencies in '58, not the least of which was the Los Angeles Police Department. Lawmen's complaints about brake fade prompted Chevy to eventually offer stouter brakes for police cruisers.*

Above: *Taking a tip from street-racing miscreants, some law-enforcement agencies in the Fifties paired a manufacturer's lightest two-door model with special high-power "police" V-8s. Here's how the formula was applied to a '58 Delray for highway patrol duty in Michigan.*

DEDICATED TO LAW ENFORCEMENT...
DESTINED FOR DUTY THROUGHOUT AMERICA

1959 CHEVROLET POLICE CARS

Right: *Chevrolet kept things simple for the cover of its 1959 police-car brochure. Fleet-vehicle catalogs were usually less flashy than their consumer-vehicle counterparts.*

With the country's ever-expanding system of high-speed interstate highways, law-enforcement agencies had an even greater need for mobility. Like most other Detroit autos, Chevrolets grew significantly throughout the Fifties and Sixties. For the most part, police departments welcomed this growth—large interiors were good for hauling both officers and suspects, and big trunks could carry lots of service-equipment necessities. While civilian cars were getting more and more glamorous, police vehicles maintained their no-nonsense functionality. Chevrolet police cars were virtually always low-line Delray, Biscayne, or maybe Bel Air models with small "dog-dish" hubcaps and minimal chrome trim.

Left and bottom: *This '66 six-cylinder Bel Air sedan wasn't originally a police car, but became one during restoration. Its decals and lights are all authentic Chicago Police Department items.*

Above: *Many folks still regard Chevy's full-size '62s as some of the finest cars in Detroit history. Illinois' finest would likely agree, especially those who patrolled the state's highways in Biscayne sedans like this one.*

1976-1986

Right: *A Nova four-door sedan with the 9C1 package graced the cover of Chevrolet's 1976 police-vehicle brochure. The Nova's compact dimensions made it ideal for patrolling in congested city traffic.*

1976 CHEVROLET POLICE VEHICLES

Though full-size four-door sedans were still the core of its law-enforcement-vehicle business, Chevrolet broadened its police-fleet offerings in the Seventies to serve agencies with more-specialized needs. The mid-sized Chevy Nova and Malibu were easier to manage in tight inner-city quarters than a full-size car, and a bit more economical too—important in the gas-crunch days of the era. Chevy's Blazer boasted fantastic off-road ability when it was equipped with four-wheel drive, and as such was a compelling choice for park/forest ranger

duty and for police departments in rugged or mountainous locales. Meanwhile, Chevrolet engineers never stopped tinkering with the full-size Impala/Caprice sedan police package to make it stronger, faster, and more comfortable. No wonder so many law-enforcement agencies kept coming back for more year after year.

Above: *Chevrolet offered a Malibu police unit in 1979 in both two- and four-door versions. It was created to replace the soon-to-be-discontinued Nova.*
Left: *Chevy touted the virtues of its '79 Blazer police unit, listing among its uses the towing of law-enforcement boat, horse, or command-post trailers—along with the obvious snow-rescue duty.*

Left: *Chevrolet's 1977-1990 full-size sedans were well-suited for police duty. Pictured here is a 1981 Impala in the markings of Warren, Michigan—hometown of the General Motors Technical Center.*

Right: *The Impala trim level was discontinued for 1986, so Chevy's full-size police package moved to the Caprice model. The example shown here is a Los Angeles County Sheriff's cruiser.*

1991-1998

Right: *The Caprice Classic got a radical redesign for 1991, with "aero-style" curves replacing the previous boxy lines. As expected, the 9C1 police package carried over.* **Far right:** *With various highway patrols running souped-up Ford Mustangs, Chevy countered with a Police Package Camaro for 1991, here fronting a "civilian" Z28 coupe.*

Middle: *All Caprice Classics, police cars included, got more-conventional rear-wheel openings and other minor styling updates for 1993.*
Bottom: *Chevy offered a Police Package for the midsize 1993 Lumina sedan as well, but officers greatly preferred the full-size Caprice for its superior strength, V-8 speed, roomier interior, and more-familiar rear-wheel-drive handling traits.*

Right: *Thanks in part to their gutsy 260-hp LT1 V-8s, the 1996 Police Package Caprices were some of the best police cars Chevrolet ever made.* **Far right top and middle:** *Chevy devised a Police Package Tahoe in 1996 to take over for the outgoing Caprice, but officers didn't like it nearly as much. The Tahoe Police Package was based on the lowest-trim-level Tahoe (as evidenced by the non-chromed, single-headlight grille), and included the usual high-output "pursuit" V-8, uprated chassis, and custom law-enforcement equipment.*

Chevrolet continued to expand its police-package offerings in the Nineties, but the full-size Caprice Classic was still far and away the most popular bowtie cop car. Chrysler pulled out of the mainstream police-car market in 1989 with the cancellation of the Dodge Diplomat/Plymouth Gran Fury, leaving only Chevy's Caprice and Ford's Crown Victoria. To the dismay of many police officers, Chevrolet dropped the Caprice line after 1996, leaving the company without a traditional rear-wheel-drive police car offering for the first time in decades.

Right: *Chevy still offered a Lumina Police Package in 1998. Though no V-8 was offered, the Lumina's available 3.8-liter V-6 produced 200 horsepower and could provide decent acceleration.*

Left: *Speeders beware! The B4C Special Service Package outfitted a 1998 Camaro for "pursuit capable" police work with heavy-duty components and Z28-spec hardware. Very few were built.*

2002-2011

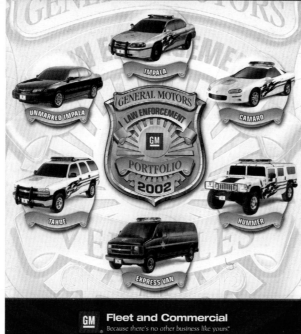

Right: *The cover of Chevrolet's 2002 police-vehicle catalog displays the wide range of special service vehicles the division offered. Light bars, push bars, equipment trays, and other specialized equipment were supplied by GM-approved second-stage manufacturers.*

Above, left, and bottom: *The 2002 Chevy Impala 9C1 Police Package had a top speed of 124 mph and included a "Surveillance Mode" switch that turned off headlamps, taillamps, and interior courtesy lights.*

Chevrolet reintroduced the Impala name-plate on a smaller front-wheel-drive chassis for the 2000 model year, and the new cars were available in police-spec 9C1 trim from the start. Though the reborn Impala was a decent performer, most police officers preferred the rear-wheel-drive layout and body-on-frame ruggedness of the departed Caprice. Ford's Crown Victoria became the default choice for most law-enforcement agencies, but Chevrolet planned to try again with the Australian-bred 2011 Caprice PPV.

Top left: *The 2010 Impala Police Package's 3.9-liter V-6 made a healthy 230 horsepower.*
Above: *Chevrolet pitched the 2010 Tahoe four-wheel-drive Special Service SUV for hazardous materials, K9, medical first responder, and tactical operations use.*

Left: *Chevrolet announced plans to re-enter the rear-wheel-drive cop-car market in fall 2010 with the 2011 Caprice PPV (Police Patrol Vehicle).*

CHAPTER EIGHT

Workhorse Wonders

Chevy first fielded its own factory-built trucks in 1931, and ever since then the company has been at the forefront of the American light-truck market. Though Chevy's trucks were typically not refreshed as often as their passenger cars, the debut of each new generation advanced the state of the art for pickup design, and was kept fresh via regular updates until the next all-new generation debuted. Over the years, these continuous improvements gradually transformed Chevrolet's rough-and-tumble workhorses into surprisingly comfortable, sophisticated vehicles—all while sacrificing none of the get-the-job-done utility that made the brand famous in the first place. And with the rise of modern-day sport-utility vehicles in the 1990s and 2000s, more Americans than ever before flocked to Chevy-truck ruggedness and reliability.

A spic-and-span trio of 1957 Chevrolet Series 3100 panel trucks stands ready for delivery duty. The ½-ton panel truck started at $2101 with standard six-cylinder power.

1933-1954

Right: *Chevy's 1933 trucks got a new louvered hood and a new 206.8-cid six. The sedan delivery is shown here.* **Far right:** *Chevy trucks were redesigned in mid-year 1936 with a new round-corner all-steel cab.* **Below left:** *This 1940 Chevy sedan delivery wears owner-added "artillery" wheels.* **Below right:** *Chevy's redesigned '41 trucks boasted in-fender sealed-beam "safety" headlamps. Here, the mainstay ½-ton pickup in the AK Series.*

Left middle: This 1950 pickup wears the optional "Nu-Vue" rear quarter windows, which increased the glass area 40 percent over the previous cab style. **Below:** *A bolder grille, one-piece windshield, and optional availability of Hydra-Matic automatic transmission made news for Chevy's 1954 truck line.*

Above: *The 1947 DeLuxe Panel Delivery could be had with accessory chrome fender trim that mimicked the look of Chevy's Fleetline passenger cars.* **Top right:** *The "Advance-Design" trucks saw little change for 1949. Standard engine was the reliable 216.5-cid "Thrift-Master" overhead-valve six with 90 hp.*

Chevrolet weathered the dark days of the Great Depression thanks in part to sales of its truck models. Styling changes for 1941 brought a distinctive new "waterfall" grille, and sales soared as the threat of war loomed. The government halted civilian truck production early in 1942 and shifted industrial resources to America's World War II effort. By the time the war ended, there was plenty of pent-up consumer demand for new vehicles. Interestingly, Chevrolet's first all-new postwar-designed vehicles were not cars but the "Advance-Design" trucks that arrived in summer 1947; Chevy had been producing trucks in limited numbers during the war, and since those truck-production lines were already in place, plans for redesigned trucks were started sooner than those for cars. The "Advance-Design" platform lasted through early 1955.

1955-1985

Right: *Even blue-collar pickups started becoming style-conscious in 1955. Leading the way was Chevy's new Cameo Carrier, which featured a unique fiberglass-skinned flush-side cargo box.* **Top right:** *A new grille and hood emblem marked Chevy's 1957 pickups, which offered their own version of the 265 V-8. This ½-ton 3100 has the optional custom cab trim and exterior chrome package.*

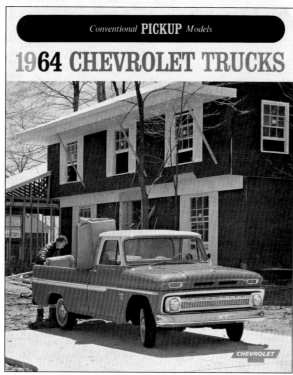

Right: *A new grille and a reworked cab that eliminated the former "wraparound" windshield were the Chevy trucks' biggest styling changes for 1964.*

C hevrolet trucks rolled through the mid-Fifties to the late-Eighties with all-new designs for 1955, '60, '67, and '73, with plenty of updates in-between to keep things fresh and up-to-date. Each new generation got more stylish and car-like than the previous design, while sacrificing none of the expected workhorse capabilities. Along the way, the milestones were numerous. The dazzling (but slow-selling) Cameo Carriers of 1955-58 introduced the slab-sided pickup beds that quickly became the industry standard. Also in '55, V-8 engines became available in addition to the stalwart sixes. Independent front suspension was introduced with the all-new 1960 models, and the torquey big block 396 V-8 was added to the options list in 1968. The evergreen 1973 basic design lasted all the way to '87.

Above: *After a full redesign for 1960, Chevy trucks saw little change for 1961. Buyers were discovering the slicker looks and extra carrying capacity of Fleetside pickups like this long-wheelbase, ½-ton Apache 10.*

Right: *Chevrolet's workhorse C-10 Stepside pickup, seen here in short-box 115-inch-wheelbase form, saw little change for 1966.* **Top right:** *Chevy pickups got a complete restyle for 1967. The basic design carried over to the '68s with only minor trim changes and the addition of sidemarker lights.* **Below:** *The little-changed 1972 Chevy pickups retained the egg-crate grille that debuted for 1971.*

Above: *A '78 Chevy pickup looked plenty handsome in Scottsdale trim. Prices started at $4493 with the long bed shown here.* **Left:** *Stepside pickup beds, as seen on this 1985 C-10 4×4, were still popular for their sporty looks.*

1988-2008

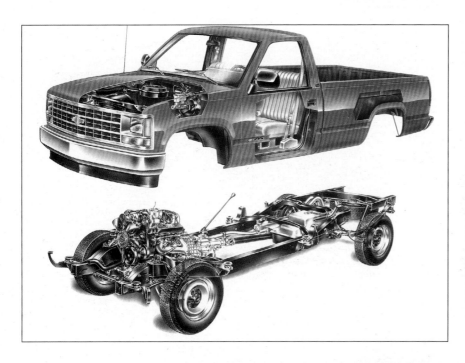

Above: *Full-size Chevy trucks began a new design generation with the 1988 rollout of fully revised light-duty pickups.* **Right:** *For 1990, Chevy released this hot 454 SS pickup with special trim, sport suspension, and a 230-hp 454 V-8 under the hood.* **Bottom:** *For 1992, the one-ton four-door Crew Cab pickup (K3500 shown) finally switched to the new pickup styling.*

The revolutionary all-new 1988 Chevrolet light trucks had a radical new look that was a bit jarring to buyers used to the 15-year-old shape of the previous design. The increased sophistication and much-improved ergonomics of the new models quickly won shoppers over, however. Pickups were becoming more and more popular with mainstream consumers during this period, and Chevy trucks were becoming more comfortable and car-like than ever before. Redesigned light-truck lineups debuted again for 1999 and 2007, and by now Chevy Silverado trucks boasted available interior trimmings and convenience features that rivaled many luxury cars. And as customers demanded more interior room, extended-cab and four-door crew-cab models supplanted traditional truck cabs as the most popular pickup body style.

Above: *Though most big Chevy trucks still sold with rear-wheel drive in 1988, demand for 4×4s was fast increasing. This photo pairs two of the several available choices, C1500s in Fleetside (left) and new Sportside trim.*

Right: *Chevy's first new-design big pickups in 11 years began rolling off the assembly line in 1999 with ½-ton 1500s and light-duty ¾-ton 2500s, all called Silverado.*

Right middle: *Plugging a gap in the big-truck field, the new 2002 Avalanche was part Suburban, part pickup, and loaded with clever features.*

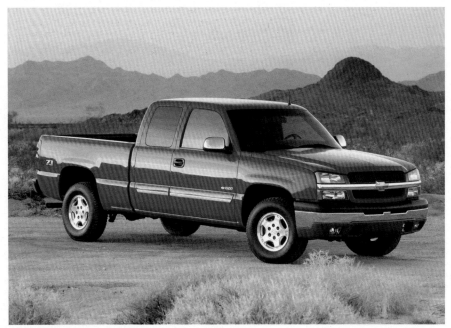

Above: *Silverados got freshened front-end styling for 2003. The Z71 Off-Road Suspension Package added $395 to the $34,405 base price of a 4WD extended-cab short bed.* **Left:** *Silverados were redesigned again in 2007 with a rugged-yet-sophisticated new look. The top engine choice in the mainstream 1500 series was a 367-hp 6.0-liter V-8.*

1936-1961 Suburban

Right and top right:
The Suburban Carryall wagon debuted for 1935, and was carried over into 1936 with minor changes. At $685, it was the priciest of Chevy's ½-ton models. Eight-passenger seating was standard, though accessing the rear seats through the two front doors or the dual rear doors must have been tricky.

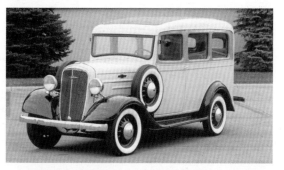

Above: *All 1936 Chevy trucks got new dashboards with relocated instruments—they were now positioned in front of the driver instead of in the center of the dash.*

Left: *Chevy's first postwar trucks closely mirrored the 1941 models. Shown here is the 1946 Model 3106 Suburban, which started at $1283.*

Right: *The Suburban Carryall continued as a two-door wagon in the new postwar "Advance-Design" truck series. A 1950 model is shown here.* **Top right:** *This 1957 Suburban is equipped with side-opening panel doors at the rear; a wagon-style liftgate/tailgate arrangement was also available.* **Below:** *Americans wouldn't go mad for four-wheel-drive trucks until the Nineties, but those who needed one in 1961 found plenty to like in this rugged Suburban.*

The first Chevrolet Suburban Carryall was conceived as a heavier-duty, truck-based alternative to the car-based, wood-bodied "depot-hack" wagons of the Thirties. The Suburban was a truly innovative vehicle; it was one of the first all-steel station wagons and is sometimes credited as "the first SUV," though that term would not appear for another 50 or so years. Essentially, Suburbans added side windows and rear seats to Chevrolet's commercial panel-delivery bodies, and for the most part they mirrored the advancements of their pickup-truck kin from year to year. Up until the Seventies, professional and commercial use was the Suburban's main forte, though that would change gradually as ordinary consumers came to appreciate the Suburban's considerable family-hauling capabilities.

CHEVROLET TRUCKS **1961** *Four-Wheel Drive Models*

1973-2010 Suburban

Right: *Starting with its 1973 redesign, the Suburban finally had two doors on each side.* **Top right:** *Suburbans rolled into 1978 with minor changes. Starting price for a ½-ton two-wheel-drive C-10 like the one shown here was $5810.*

Left: *As ever, Chevrolet's 1987 Suburbans had the power and stamina for most every need. These king-size haulers were popular tow vehicles—especially in Texas, where they now outsold many cars.*

Right: *Like Chevrolet's heavy-duty trucks, Suburbans finally adopted Chevy's latest big-pickup chassis and styling for 1992.* **Top right:** *After adopting the new GMT800 platform for 2000, Suburbans were little changed for 2001. Shown here is the heavy-duty 2500 LS model.*

Below: *The next generation of Chevy full-sized SUVs went on sale in 2006 as early 2007 models. The Avalanche, Suburban, and Tahoe (L to R) all shared the same platform.* **Bottom:** *This 2010 Suburban LT wears the $1535 Z71 off-road package, which included skid plates and chrome side steps.*

Suburbans took a huge step toward mainstream popularity with the redesigned 1973 models, in part because they were now easier to get in and out of. Up until 1966, Suburbans only had two side doors, and from 1967 to '72 there were only three (the rear door was on the passenger side only). The '73s had four side doors, and for buyers who needed even more cargo-hauling and towing capacity, a ¾-ton model with available 454-cubic-inch big-block power was newly available. The basic 1973 design lasted until 1992, when all-new Suburbans adopted the platform of Chevy's new-for-1988 light trucks. Redesigns occurred again for 2000 and 2007, but Suburbans always maintained their head-of-the-class size and hauling prowess. Volatile gas prices in the late 2000s caused many mainstream consumers to seek smaller, more economical vehicles, but Suburbans remained a terrific value for those who truly needed their rarely matched combination of passenger room and comfort, available four-wheel drive, and heavy-duty towing ability.

1969-2005 Blazer

Right: *Chevy answered the Jeep CJ and Ford Bronco with the new-for-1969 Blazer. First-year production totaled 4935 units, all with four-wheel drive.*

Below: *The compact S-10 Blazer debuted for 1983 as a logical spin-off of the new-for-1982 S-10 small pickup.*

Top left: *Blazers naturally shared in 1973's light-truck redesign. A "Sports Cap" roof was $313 extra.* **Left:** *A catalytic converter was among the few changes to the 1979 Blazer, but sales remained strong.*

The Blazer joined Chevrolet's model lineup in 1969 as an open-air off-road fun machine with a lift-off fiberglass top. Over the years, the nameplate underwent quite a metamorphosis. After spending all of the Seventies as a full-size two-door machine, the Blazer family was expanded in 1983 to include the S-10 Blazer, a junior-sized variant based on Chevy's smart new S-10 compact pickup. In 1990, a four-door model joined the S-10 Blazer line. In 1995, the full-size Blazer was renamed Tahoe, and it too gained a four-door model. With that, the Blazer nameplate was now used solely on Chevy's compact SUV models, which survived until the 2005 model year.

Right: *Blazers soldiered on all the way to 1991 using the basic 1973-vintage design, but were regularly revitalized with minor updates.* **Top right:** *Like their Suburban counterparts, the 1992 Blazers switched to the new design that Chevy light pickups had been using since 1988. A 1993 model is shown here.*

Above: *Chevy's compact SUV dropped its S-10 prefix to become simply the "Blazer" for 1995 and shared its basic design with the 1994 S-10 compact pickup. Both two- and four-door models were available.* **Left:** *The long-running compact Blazer appeared for the last time in 2005. Pictured here is a 4WD model with the off-road-oriented ZR2 option package.*

1959-1986 El Camino

Left: *After a three-year hiatus, El Camino migrated to the intermediate Chevelle platform for 1964. The 1965 models got a new grille and other trim changes.*
Middle: *After a complete restyle for 1968, the El Camino was little changed for 1969. Prices started at $2550 with six, $2640 with base V-8.*

Above: *Answering Ford's 1957-58 Ranchero, Chevy's new 1959 El Camino was basically a two-door wagon with a pickup box instead of an enclosed cargo deck. Billed as "combining ultra style with utility," it effectively replaced the slow-selling Cameo Carrier; 22,246 were built.*

Bottom left: *El Camino got its own "Colonnade" styling for 1973, with the obligatory 5-mph bumpers.* **Below:** *El Camino Classics could get this unusual two-tone paint scheme in 1977.*

Right: *El Caminos were redesigned for 1978 along with the newly downsized Malibu. Engine choices ranged from a 3.3-liter V-6 to the 350-cid V-8. Shown here is the uplevel Conquista trim.*

Below: *El Caminos got a new four-headlight grille for 1982, and were continued mostly unchanged through 1987. Standard 1985 models like this one started at $8933.* **Bottom:** *In 1986, Chevy dealers sold an El Camino SS fitted with a "droop snoot" that mimicked the nose on the company's popular Monte Carlo SS.*

El Caminos debuted for 1959 on Chevy's full-size car platform, and were carried over into 1960 with the expected styling changes. The model was then dropped, only to be reborn in 1964 on the new Chevelle/Malibu midsize chassis. The El Camino's intriguing combination of passenger-car style and road manners and pickup-truck utility won over many shoppers. Plus, its close kinship with its Chevelle/Malibu parent meant that El Camino offered many of the same desirable trim options and engine choices, most notably the flashy Super Sport package and the big-block 396 and 454 powerplants. However, as pickup trucks got more luxurious in the Eighties, the El Camino began to seem like more of a compromise than a solution. Sales began to dwindle, and the last El Camino came off the line in late 1987, with several hundred reportedly sold as 1988 models.

Index

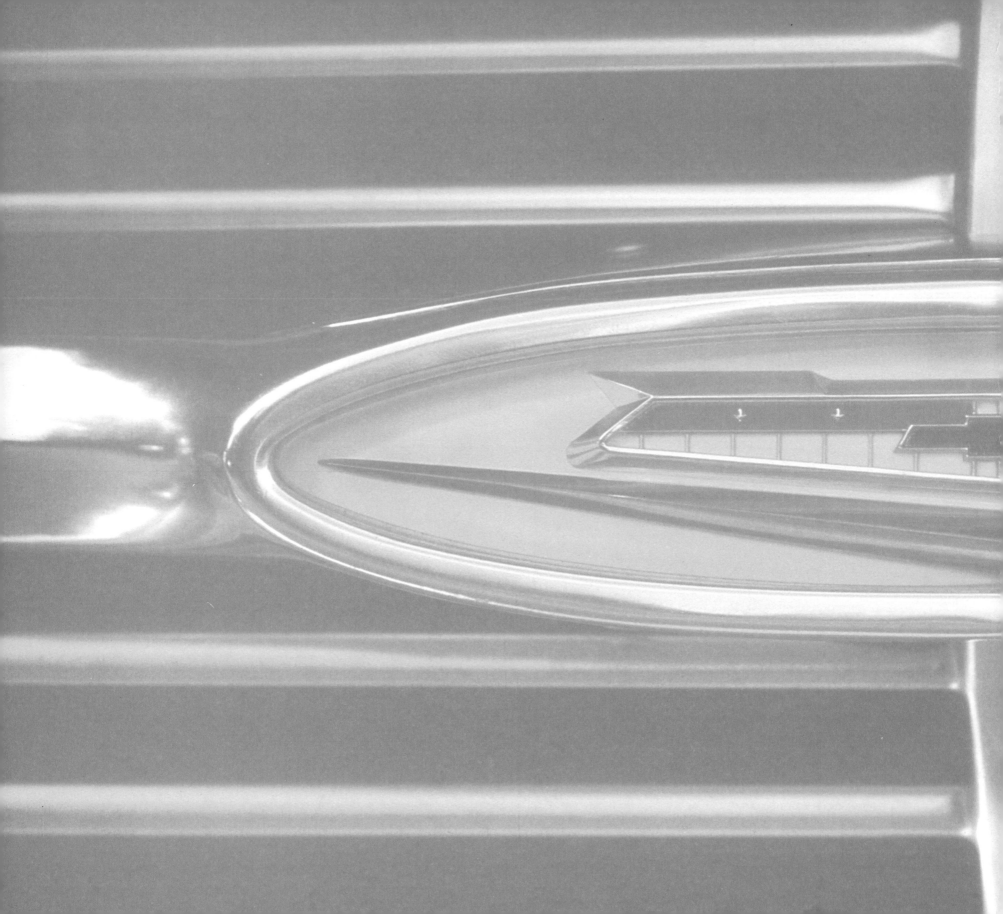